OUTSIDE IN

Mike Breen

Scripture Union

130 City Road, London EC1V 2NJ

© Mike Breen 1993

First published 1993

ISBN 0 86201 811 0

British Library Cataloguing-in-Publication Data.
A catalogue record for this book is available from the
British Library.

All Bible quotations in this publication
are from the Holy Bible, New International version.
Copyright © 1973, 1978, 1984 International Bible
Society.
Published by Hodder and Stoughton.

Phototypeset by Intype, London.
Printed and bound in Great Britain by
Cox and Wyman Ltd, Reading.
Cover by Ross Advertising.
Book design by
Illustrations by Sharyn Troughton.

Contents

Introduction

Young people are the most valuable human resources in the world today. Overall, the church has failed to grasp this or do anything about it for decades. There are, of course, notable exceptions both at a local and national level. But the fact remains that the church is desperately short of young people and appears to have little idea of what it should do to rectify it.

If there was any doubt about this the English Church Census has driven home this very point with real force. In general we belong to a church in Britain that is getting smaller and older. Membership goes down as membership age goes up. If we do not address this situation, yet another generation of young people will be lost and without hope, with little chance of ever hearing the gospel. I believe the situation today is as desperate as it has ever been and probably even more desperate than we are prepared to admit.

It is with this situation in mind that this book is offered. The book seeks to address two basic questions:

- How do we begin to reach out to young people effectively with the gospel?
- How do we continue to do this once we have begun?

Most of us have limited resources and personnel at our disposal and the challenge of youth work is often greatest where churches are the smallest (the inner cities and rural communities of our nation). So, the question of how to reach out and how to continue needs to be answered with realism, taking these limitations into account. This book is written from the perspective that if we take on the message and the methods of the New Testament we will be able to meet the challenge of living out the mission of Jesus to young people.

This is intended to be a workbook: to get the best use of it you should try to get your youth work team to do the exercises together.

In writing this book I have used a lot of the methodology from my book, *Growing the Smaller Church* (Marshalls, 1992).

Communicating across the cultural divide

Sally Watling, a local youth worker, ran screaming across the church car park pursued by three young men shouting at the top of their voices. When she got to the high chain link fence and realised she could go no further she turned to meet her pursuers. Curling herself up into a ball she gave a wail of resignation.

The curtains in the old people's sheltered accommodation on the other side of the can park were twitching furiously, as with some anxiety, the residents watched the events taking place below. By now Sally's pursuers had collapsed into fits of giggles and Sally, also laughing, was making her way back to the church door where the trainer was now calling people to reassemble. As I walked from the vicarage to the church across the car park I waved to the old folks and shouted that it was just another youth workers' training day!

The Grunters and the Farbacks

The game we were playing is called 'Two Tribes'. We were using it to help us understand the difficulties of communicating cross-culturally and from one world view to another.

It is obvious to anyone involved in Christian youth work that an understanding of youth culture and world view is central to any attempt to reach out to young people. The good news of the kingdom that Jesus brought is best communicated when we understand the position of the people we are seeking to reach. If we want to proclaim the gospel we must speak 'on their level' if we are to get a hearing.

Whenever I have been involved in the training of youth workers I have tried to take this fact into account. In teaching others how to communicate across age and culture barriers, Two Tribes has always proved helpful. It invents two distinct cultures and languages, brings them into contact and then asks them to interact. The two tribes are called 'The Grunters' and 'The Farbacks'.

In the game the Farbacks are a highly gregarious tribe of people who spend much of their time socialising with one another. The basic rules of their society are that they always welcome and greet one another warmly, using verbal and physical expressions of affection. They are always chatting, hugging, shaking hands and generally passing the time of day with one another. They love to play games, the most common being the card game happy families, or tick-tack-toe. Everybody plays these games on equal terms, except when the game is played with the designated leader of the group, who is always allowed to win. The Farbacks value talking, touching, playing and believe in a hierarchical society.

The Grunters are quite different. They are a people of few words and spend most of their time bartering for different coloured pieces of paper. Once a person has settled on a particular colour of paper that they want to collect they barter with other Grunters to try to collect as many pieces as possible. A barter is initiated by one Grunter scratching himself in the presence of another Grunter. If the barter is accepted the other Grunter scratches in return. The barter is conducted by each Grunter making plain which colour of paper they are after by using the first two letters of the colour in the form of a grunt. A Grunter looking for blue would say 'bl', someone looking for green would say 'gr'. In establishing how many pieces are involved in the barter, the Grunter will hold up fingers, sometimes quite aggressively, to indicate what they think is the going rate. As far as anyone has been able to ascertain, the Grunters have no recognised leadership structure. But they do have a very strong taboo about touching. An uninvited touch is extremely offensive.

Two Tribes begins by dividing the group into two halves, with each half placed in separate rooms. They are then introduced to their new tribe and culture without any reference to the other cultural group that they will soon be meeting. Each tribe is given a few minutes to get used to their new identity and is then encouraged to send out an 'anthropologist' to investigate the other group. On their return the anthropologist is encouraged to share with their tribe their impressions of the other group from the viewpoint of their own new found culture.

Invariably the Grunters decide that they do not want to meet the Farbacks and want to get on with bartering in peace. The Farbacks, gregarious to the last, decide en masse to go and meet the other tribe and see if they will play tick-tack-toe with them. The meeting of the Two Tribes is usually explosive and hardly ever promotes harmony and understanding!

Sally, a Grunter running across the church car park, pursued by a group of hooting Farbacks trying to touch her, is an example of just how explosive the meeting can be.

The game highlights the need for sensitivity, understanding and insight when communicating across cultural barriers. If we want to reach out and work with young people it would be good to bear this mind. Just as in the game each team sent out an 'anthropologist' to observe the other group, we must begin in the same way. If we want to be effective youth workers reaching out with the love of God to a generation of young people, we will be most effective if we begin with observation. Good youth workers always start as anthropologists!

Adults and young people

There is strong evidence that even though adults and young people are part of the same society, they interact as two separate cultures. In fact it is probably more accurate to say that young people represent a subculture of the larger group to which they belong. But for our purposes here it is only necessary to recognise that a cultural barrier exists. This invisible barrier creates unseen tensions which can have an explosive effect if they are ignored.

How many parents discover that the children they have raised appear, at the advent of puberty, to become different people? Communication becomes difficult; the world, once so ordered, is suddenly turned upside-down. Instead of peace and happiness there is strife and tears. The young people no longer fulfil the expectations of the adults around them. They no longer conform to the same standards of behaviour expected of them and their lifestyle conflicts with that of the adult world around them.

Put adults and young people together and conflict is never far away. Young people will say they are not actually looking for conflict with adults, but are only wanting to experiment and satisfy their curiosity. However when these experiments, usually done in secret, are discovered, conflict usually results.

Take the example of some friends of ours, who returning from an evening out, heard their two teenage daughters laughing and giggling in the back garden. Pleased that the arguments earlier in the day between the two had obviously been resolved, the parents decide to add to the fun by creeping up and surprising the girls. They found them smoking cigarettes and acting around. Their hopes and expectations were dashed and underlying conflicts soon surfaced!

GET GOING!

Understanding young people

From what we have seen in this chapter there appear to be basic problems of communication between adults and young people. If we are to be effective in building relationships with young people we must discover ways of understanding them as they are.

An understanding on youth subculture can be achieved by:

- Observation
- Reflection
- Discussion

We need exposure to the world of young people, but we also need an understanding of that world. **Observation** of young people, spending time with young people and talking to them in settings that are natural for them will begin to help us gain a perspective on youth culture. The information we obtain through this observation will become more valuable to us if we are able to develop a simple method of **reflection** – thinking through – what it all means. If we take our reflections and share them through **discussion** with others who have gone through the same process of observation and reflection, our knowledge, understanding and insight of young people will be significantly increased.

Observation
To observe and meet young people in natural settings:

- Watch and listen to young people on a bus, in a cinema queue or pub, at a football match, music concert, youth club etc.
- Talk to young people in any of the above settings, using the questions in the next section. You will need permission to do this in some situations (eg youth club). Also ask your local secondary school if you can come and meet a group of young people, with a view to understanding their needs and aspirations. If you say this is because you are considering setting up a youth project they will often comply.
- View the media that is aimed at young people; the music, films, magazines and television programmes which are specifically geared to the youth market. Make a special point of reading the problem page or watching the agony aunt section on TV.
- Are there other things that you can think of that will give you exposure to youth culture?

Reflection
During and after the process of observation, these questions

need to be considered:

- What are the strongly held beliefs of the young people you meet?
- How have their parents taught them to behave?
- What do the young people regard as major offences to their moral code?
- What do they do in a crisis?
- Who are the trend setters?
- What are their greatest fears?
- What is considered to be wisdom, and who are the wisdom givers?
- What is expressed in the art forms of youth culture?
- What aspects of youth culture are most resistant to change?

If you are able to answer these questions to your own satisfaction you will begin to have an insight into young people, their culture and worldview.

Discussion

Now take your observations and conclusions and share and discuss them with someone else who has gone through the same process of observation and reflection. At the end of your discussion it will be necessary to test some of your conclusions by briefly going through the process of observation and reflection again. A good youth worker never stops observing, reflecting and discussing.

Where does 'youth culture' come from?

Although the division between young and old has always been there (even Plato reflected upon it) it seems to have become more obvious in the last few decades. It seems as though the development of youth culture in the Western world over the last forty years is directly related to affluence and education.

Education

In the modern world 'information is power', and young people have more information than anyone. Modern educational methods see to it that in general young people coming through school know more about the academic subjects that they study than their parents who were educated perhaps twenty or thirty years earlier. In general young people stay in full time education longer and have more information at their fingertips than any generation before them.

It's bad enough for most parents that teenagers are seeking independence and therefore challenge their authority. But when they realise that young people 'know' more than them and that their role as elders providing wisdom and direction is unwanted, real problems start! Unlike past centuries when young people were dependent on their parents and elders for the skills to survive and to earn a living, young people today learn new things which have little relationship to the wisdom of the past. Paradoxically, this education which is the cause of so much conflict is encouraged by adults and parents. How many times have we heard, 'I want them to have opportunities I never had'?

Affluence

Growing affluence in society has provided these educational opportunties, but has also provided the opportunity for young people to express their desire for independence. In the past, independence was only a dream; today it seems within everyone's reach. In fact society at large seems to encourage this quest for independence. There are few of the structures and social sanctions present in society which at one time held society together. Morality, stable communities and family life are either optional or definitely discouraged. Success and prosperity are most important. Affluence has led to greater educational opportunities and greater independence for us all.

Images of youth

When we decide to make a study of young people – understanding their worldview so that we can communicate on their level – we should not be too easily influenced by everything we see. Today industry and commerce, marketing and finance, all see young people as the single most important consumer group. If the advertisements were to be believed, everyone wants to be young. 'Young' means healthy, sexy, worry free and happy.

If we took the advertising industry seriously we would think that everyone wants to be young. But there is another image of young people. In contrast to the advertising industry the news media – papers, television, etc – present young people in a rather different light. Young people are the criminals, the hooligans, the thugs and muggers. This image has been so effectively presented that many old people live in fear of what young people might do to them.

Adults find young people challenging, even intimidating. How many adults have not felt apprehensive when they have turned a corner and walked into a group of young people hanging around with apparently nothing to do? Young people seem to represent a threat just by their presence. This apparent threat is often groundless, based more on media hype than hard facts. We need to be careful whose view of young people we share, and whether our current understanding is based on reality.

Symptoms and causes

In their search for independence and their apparent freedom to do what they want despite the consequences, young people have problems that everyone recognises, but for which no one seems to have an answer. Parents and adults feel the need to control young people, fearing the consequences of irresponsible behaviour. They want to 'clip their wings', realising that too much freedom would lead to disaster. Young people resist the interference in their lives and so the problems continue. But these problems are only a symptom of a much deeper problem.

Young people searching through their teenage years for identity and a sense of meaning, turn away from what they see as parental control to peer groups and sexual experimentation, to find what they are looking for. Who they are, what they mean and how much they are worth are the main questions to be answered. If they are unequipped to answer these questions, inner conflicts develop which find expression in their conflicts with others. The fearsome experience of having both inner and outer conflicts lead some to try to escape. Escapes can be found in various kinds of fun, pleasure and personal gratification Music, sex, alcohol, drugs and parties are all attempts, some more legitimate than others, to find answers to the pressures of being young. Young people may become victims of their own search for value and significance. They need answers and are often ready to listen to anyone who says they have a solution.

GET GOING! ————————————————

By this stage it should be apparent that youth culture is supported by a particular worldview – a way of seeing the world. Everyone has a worldview. If we did not we would not be able to survive. A worldview enables a person to understand and operate within the world in which they live. There are many different worldviews and the worldviews of young people, though broadly similar to that of the adult world around them, will have specific characteristics.

Having completed the observation, reflection and discussion section you can now achieve a better understanding of the worldview that supports youth culture and weigh its relative strengths and weaknesses.

You can ask whether the worldview provides:

- **Explanation** – does it explain how and why the world exists and is as it is?
- **Evaluation** – does it provide a way of judging between right and wrong?
- **Affirmation** – does it provide encouragement and hope in times of crisis?
- **Integration** – does it encompass most of life's experiences?
- **Assimilation** – does it easily accept new information, knowledge and experience?

These questions are quite complex, but nevertheless reveal whether a worldview will be successful or not in the long run. Some worldviews from the past have crumbled because they have not been able to answer one or more of these questions. For instance the 'flat earthers' saw their worldview destroyed as Columbus sailed round the world. Also some had their worldview and faith in God shattered during the world wars because they had no substantial way of receiving encouragement and hope for the future.

The church and young people

The church has the answers that the young people seek but the church and Christian youth work is largely in the hands of adults. So we, like everyone else, have all sorts of problems in seeking to reach out and communicate the gospel.

But for us there is an answer. It is seen in the life of Jesus and summed up in one word – incarnation. Incarnation means 'becoming flesh'. God – who created and sustains the world – took on human flesh in his Son Jesus, in order to communicate with people and redeem the cosmos. We take on others' flesh when we 'get inside their skin' and see and feel the world as they do.

In the letter to the Philippians Paul talks about the incarnation when he says:

> Your attitude should be the same as that of Christ Jesus: Who, being in very nature God, did not consider equality with God something to be grasped, But made himself nothing, taking the very nature of a servant, being made in human likeness. And being found in appearance as a man, he humbled himself and became obedient to death – even death on a cross! (Philippians 2:5–8).

Jesus made himself nothing, a servant, humble, obedient, crucified. This description is almost incredible when we consider that Paul is talking about the eternal Son of God. If we are to be followers of Jesus and fulfil the mission to the world that he has given us, we must begin where he began and take on the flesh of others, getting inside the skin of those we seek to reach. We have a calling to preach the good news, but *proclamation* must begin with *identification* and *identification* is only possible through *incarnation*.

To reach young people we must communicate as an 'insider' and not appear to be shouting at them from a distance.

Incarnation and identification

Beccy, a youth worker at All Saints, Brixton Hill, has discovered along with others in the youth team how much it costs to identify with the young people.

One Sunday evening a girl, whom we will call Fiona, came to church on the recommendation of a friend who had told her that she needed to get to know God. After the service, still visibly moved by what she had experienced, Fiona began to talk through with Beccy her sudden and new found awareness of God's presence.

Over the next week Fiona came every day and spent the whole day with Beccy, opening up more and more and sharing more deeply about her life each time they met. Real trust developed between the two of them and Fiona's confidence to share the pain and difficulties that she faced increased. She told Beccy that she had never told anyone before of some of the experiences she had had. When, two weeks later, her elder brother was dying of chronic heroin addiction, she turned to Beccy to help her understand.

Beccy explained that the wrong things in the world were there because of people's sinful and selfish nature and because there was a devil – God's enemy – who manipulated these things to his own end. Fiona decided to ask God to change her first and in so doing, make her an agent of change in the lives of others.

Through all of this Beccy chose to share Fiona's pain and sadness. More than once she would go to others in the youth team in tears, her emotions shredded by what she had just heard. But something was happening: Fiona was finding a friend she could rely on and Beccy was discovering again how God supports us as we reach out to others.

Fiona decided to start a Christian discipleship course with Beccy, which she would start the next time they met. The first thing that became obvious when they met for the first session was that Fiona could not read. Beccy had to read slowly through the notes and Bible until Fiona could memorise what she needed to learn.

Things continued well until a few days later when she was thrown out of her family home and into council care. But changes had already begun to show in Fiona's life. Her frequent fights and violent reactions to others, which had contributed to her being placed in a school for children with special needs, began to moderate. She was soon out of council care again and living with her sister, who like others, saw the changes taking place. She was also miraculously healed of kidney stones after Beccy prayed for her. All of these things served to encourage her to continue on the path she had begun.

Fiona continues to need regular contact and constant friendship as God continues to heal the abuse and pain of her past. But, because one person took the time to identify with her and her needs, unstoppable changes have begun to take place in her life. God is able to communicate His love most effectively when we use his methods. They begin with incarnation and identification.

Identification and proclamation
Identification has less to do with techniques in communication and more to do with spending our time and energy in understanding young people from their point of view. Effective communication using 'up to date' and 'trendy' techniques may be legitimate if they are the results of identification, but should never be relied upon when there is no relationship to support them.

For example, multi-media Christian roadshows are great if those presenting the gospel in this way know the young people and how they think and feel. But techniques in communication can never replace relationships formed out of hours spent together. I have been to roadshows when there is a long term commitment to the young people and relationships are central, and to one off events. I know which produces the best results! When we know young people we will communicate effectively. But until we know them, we never will.

I can remember times when I, and others with me, have spent hundreds of hours and hundreds of pounds setting up a 'youth event' designed to reach young people. Invariably these events have not achieved the results sought. More often than not this is because the time spent in preparing the event would have been better spent in developing relationships.

'Close Encounters' was one such event. We transformed the inside of a church to look like the flight deck of a spaceship, using computer graphics, lighting and all sorts of electronic wizardry. We produced the right effect. The publicity, which was excellent, went out, but the people didn't come in. As I reviewed the event afterwards I could not understand why God did not send more people to hear the gospel. Only as I thought and prayed it through did I realise what had gone wrong – we had short cut on relationships and concentrated on techniques. If we rely on 'methods' rather than relationships in our communication of the gospel we will become facile and shallow and will never see God bring about radical changes in people's lives.

GET GOING!

We have gained insight into the youth culture and the world-views that supports it. Now, we need to determine our response. This comes in three stages –

- **Planning**
- **Communicating**
- **Acting**

Fig 1.1   The learning loop

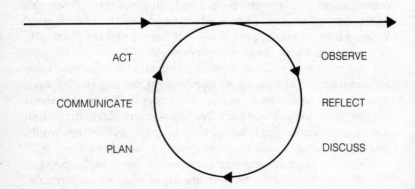

ACT   OBSERVE

COMMUNICATE   REFLECT

PLAN   DISCUSS

If you combine these three things with the three initial steps of observing, reflecting and discussing, you create what I call 'the learning loop' (see Fig. 1.1).

Having *observed*, *reflected* and *discussed* we are now able to *plan* a response, *communicate* this plan to others who will share in its execution and corporately *act* on what we now know and understand. We will return to the learning loop in a later chapter.

The 'How to Respond' flow diagram (Fig 1.2, page 20) will help in developing a response to young people.

Now try it yourself using the empty flow diagram (Fig 1.3, page 21).

(This material owes a great deal to *The Clash of the Worlds* by David Burnett, [MARC Europe, 1990].)

According to a recent English Church Census, fewer young people go to church and publicly own the Christian faith than ever before. But young people are still seeking spiritual answers to their everyday questions. The challenge for us is to reach out with the answers that God provides in a way that allows him to speak to the questions, needs and concerns directly and powerfully.

The gospel is the only truly effective means of change available to a human being. If we are to communicate this good news, which is the power of God to transform and rescue people, we must begin where God himself begins – with incarnation.

I am certain that God is totally committed to reaching out to young people in Britain today. But he is also committed to his methods. If only we would allow him to act and speak through us in the way that he wants to, we would be able to reach young people. An incredible transformation in our society would take place.

Fig 1.2 **How to Respond (I)**

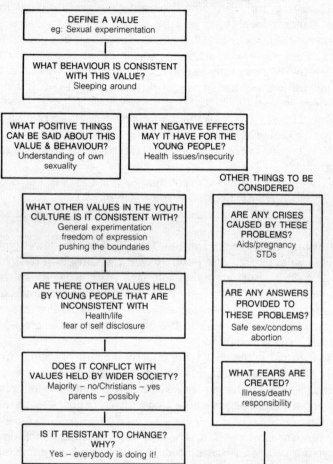

DEFINE A VALUE
eg: Sexual experimentation

WHAT BEHAVIOUR IS CONSISTENT
WITH THIS VALUE?
Sleeping around

WHAT POSITIVE THINGS
CAN BE SAID ABOUT THIS
VALUE & BEHAVIOUR?
Understanding of own
sexuality

WHAT NEGATIVE EFFECTS
MAY IT HAVE FOR THE
YOUNG PEOPLE?
Health issues/insecurity

OTHER THINGS TO BE
CONSIDERED

WHAT OTHER VALUES IN THE YOUTH
CULTURE IS IT CONSISTENT WITH?
General experimentation
freedom of expression
pushing the boundaries

ARE ANY CRISES
CAUSED BY THESE
PROBLEMS?
Aids/pregnancy
STDs

ARE THERE OTHER VALUES HELD
BY YOUNG PEOPLE THAT ARE
INCONSISTENT WITH
Health/life
fear of self disclosure

ARE ANY ANSWERS
PROVIDED TO
THESE PROBLEMS?
Safe sex/condoms
abortion

DOES IT CONFLICT WITH
VALUES HELD BY WIDER SOCIETY?
Majority – no/Christians – yes
parents – possibly

WHAT FEARS ARE
CREATED?
Illness/death/
responsibility

IS IT RESISTANT TO CHANGE?
WHY?
Yes – everybody is doing it!

THESE THREE BOXES OFTEN PROVIDE A WAY
IN FOR CARING CHRISTIAN INVOLVEMENT AND A
COMMUNICATION OF THE GOSPEL. BUT WE
NEED TO BE SURE IN COMMUNICATING THE
GOSPEL THAT WE AFFIRM THE STRENGTHS OF
THEIR WORLD VIEW AS WELL AS EXPOSE
THEIR WEAKNESSES

Fig 1.3 **How to Respond (II)**

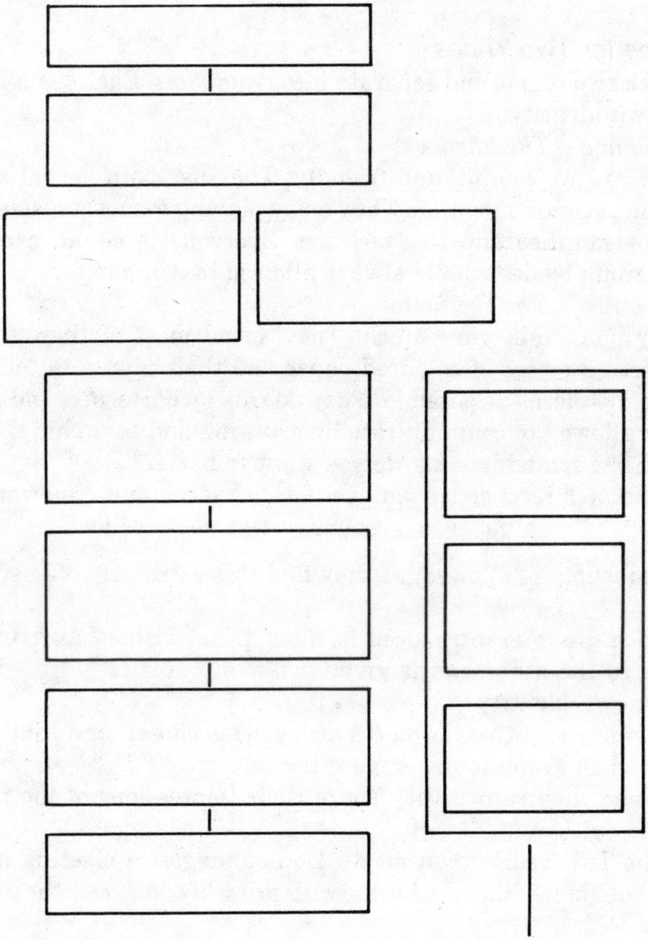

ACTION EXTRA ─────────────────

Rules for Two Tribes

1 Pick two teams and separate into two rooms. Each team has its own identity:

Team one – The Farbacks

They are welcoming and friendly. They use both verbal and physical communication. They enjoy playing games, especially happy families and tick-tack-toe. Everyone is equal, except the group leader who is always allowed to win games.

Team two – The Grunters

They don't talk very much. They spend most of their time collecting pieces of coloured paper and their aim is to collect as many pieces as possible. They do this by bartering, and are only allowed to communicate by grunting and scratching.

(a) First scratch means 'do you want to barter?'
(b) Scratch returned means 'yes I do, what colour do you want?'
  (c) 'bl' = blue 'gr' = green 'r' = red 'ye' = yellow

No touching is allowed, as they find this extremely offensive.

2 Each group is introduced to their 'tribe' without any reference to the other and is given a few minutes to get used to their own identity.

3 A representative (an anthropologist) is chosen and sent out from each group to investigate the other.

4 When they return they share their impressions of the new found culture.

5 The Two Tribes then meet! (Do not suggest a meeting if at all possible – the Farbacks will probably suggest the idea themselves.)

6 After mayhem has subsided allow both groups, now out of role, to discuss their experiences and reflect on its relevance to their work.

Types of youth work

Historically, the church has been in the forefront of attempts to respond to the needs of young people. In fact, it would be true to say that Christians have pioneered most forms of youth work we see today. In general the work falls into three areas: structured/uniformed, semi-structured/informal and unstructured/informal. The church has led the way in each of these, and still makes a vital contribution even though government and secular voluntary organisations have taken over many of the responsibilities.

Structured/uniformed

During the nineteenth and early twentieth centuries, Christians pioneered work among young people through the Sunday school movement and the uniformed organisations (the Scouts and Boys Brigade etc). They developed as a result of the need for education and recreation among the large numbers of young people in the church. Their development mirrored the society of the day which valued structure, stability, status and a 'given' moral code.

This style and these values continue today in the structured youth work seen in many Sunday schools, youth fellowships such as Pathfinder, and Covenanters and uniformed youth programmes such as Scouts and Guides. Together these programmes and organisations have been highly effective in discipling new generations of young people to take up responsible adult membership in the church and so continue the witness of Christ to the nation.

This type of work seems to work most successfully in environments where families and communities maintain a degree of structure and stability, and where the values and morality of previous generations persist. The style has been criticised for being too middle class and only effective in the suburbs. Apart from being unfair, this is also inaccurate. It is only true insofar as the so called 'middle class' and suburban communities continue to value the structure, stability and morality of the past. It has been effective in the lives of thousands, and makes a major contribution to what God is doing among young people.

Val Swanborough, a church warden of All Saints Church, Brixton Hill, was for twenty years the Brown Owl of the local Brownie pack. Val would describe herself as an unlikely youth worker, but has nevertheless influenced the lives of many hundreds of young people through her conscientious work.

Her real work was done outside the pack meetings as she built relationships with the girls, spending time with them and running informal Bible studies for those who wanted to come. This emphasis may have meant that Brownie law and procedure were not followed to the letter – one girl sent her a Christmas card and addressed it to Brown Ale! – but the lives of many have undoubtedly been influenced.

The structure, familiar programme served as an opportunity for Val to develop the sort of trusting relationships that produced young disciples of Jesus. In the last few years, Val has assimilated her pack into the other areas of youth work at All Saints. This did not prove to be a problem, because it was the relationship, not the organisation, that mattered most.

When those involved in this kind of work concentrate on relationships and a personal witness to Christ instead of structure and organisation, successful work usually follows. Youth work that relies on structure and a strong identity and ethos can be effective in attracting large numbers of young people, particularly if it is done well. It seems foolish not to use the opportunities that this provides to contact, reach out, befriend and disciple young people.

There are, of course, many thousands of young people who will never be touched by this approach. Other programmes and approaches will be needed for them. But instead of trying to create a universally effective form of youth work, our motto should be 'different horses for different courses' – something which the apostle Paul passionately believed in: 'To the weak I am weak, to win the weak. I have become all things to all men so that by all possible means I might save some. I do this for the sake of the gospel that I may share in its blessings' (1 Corinthians 9:22–23).

Whichever approach we use, good practice is the same. Good practice is based on the right principles. These underlie good youth work whatever form it takes. The principles which make for an effective Christian scout master are the same as those which make a good detached youth worker working on the streets of a large city.

Semi-structured/informal

This type of youth work is best exemplified by club-based activities. Open youth clubs, which usually have an open membership and voluntary programme, developed during the fifties and sixties as a response to the burgeoning youth culture. Initially there was talk of 'youth bunkers' and 'keeping them off the streets', but soon ideas developed which emphasised a creative approach to social education. The youth club movement, again pioneered by Christians, probably represents the most important development in youth work this century.

Working in this context, youth workers have developed priorities and aims which are now universally accepted by both Christian and secular organisations. Most agree that youth work is to do with 'social education' – enabling young people to develop to maturity as they are encouraged to grow physically, emotionally, socially and spiritually. How this is done is open to debate and Christians need to remain distinctive. But the aims remain largely the same.

As population dropped, affluence increased and greater choice in the use of leisure time developed through the sixties, seventies and eighties, causing membership to drop, youth clubs were put under pressure to continue to attract the numbers they did at first. Government and voluntary funded clubs, which represented a large investment in buildings, staff and equipment, needed to be used effectively to justify the expense. Nevertheless open youth clubs still represent an important option for young people. Clubs are particularly effective where communities exist that do not offer the variety of leisure and recreation found in large cities. Youth clubs still provide the cornerstone of provision for many young people in the community.

A lot of time and energy has gone into developing club programmes that attract young people to come in, but the competition from the leisure and recreation industry is fierce. Many youth workers find the programme a continuous pressure, and battle to put on the sort of programmes young people want. I remember vividly the anxiety of trying to produce a programme which club members would find attractive. I also remember the growing sense of desperation which accompanied each failure. Eventually, confronted by a group of club members who said they didn't want to get involved with my new programme because it was boring, I resorted to pleading and condemnation: 'Don't you realise how hard I've worked to put this on? You're so ungrateful!' The reply really stung: 'You sound just like my mum!'

These and other similar experiences began to change the way I thought about youth club work and youth work in general. My club work in the East End of London and downtown Cambridge has shown me that it takes more than a good programme to attract young people. Again, relationships are the key. Where youth workers spend time and energy (often outside club hours) building relationships, young people come. Often you find that these relationships multiply and before long you have a crowd. Nothing attracts a crowd better than a crowd! The club programmes are secondary to this process of relationship building and are often incidental or irrelevant to the real work going on. The girls' loos are always a good example of this! No programmes are provided in the loos and yet hours are spent there, talking over problems and concerns. Because the loos are a private and safe environment to which boys and men have no access, discussions about the opposite sex are common. Probably more problems are sorted out here than anywhere else in the club.

Again, not all young people are reached, and perhaps clubs and similar activities are in decline, but they still represent an important provision for many young people. Wherever the right principles are practised, valuable work is always done.

Unstructured/informal

As club-based provision developed, a group began to be identified in some circles by the unfortunate title 'the unclubbables'. Often, for reasons of deprivation and alienation, this group of young people were never going to make their way into any organisation, whether it was voluntary or not.

To reach them, 'detached work' developed. The objectives were to fulfil the normal youth work aims through contact with these young people in their own surroundings. For instance, to reach the young homeless population of London means more than providing clubs and hostels for them. Detached workers seek to befriend and empower young people to make the choices that will change their lives.

Often the work seems like 'one step forward, two steps back', but occasionally real breakthroughs take place. Charles was a good example of this. When I first met him he was asking for money outside the Co-Op. The little kids of the area called him 'smelly'. He lived in an overcrowded squat with poor sanitation – one of the factors that contributed to his distinctive aroma. After two years and many hundreds of hours, Charles' life began to turn around. By the end of our time together he was helping out at the summer playscheme in his free time from work. One of my most vivid memories is of him sitting with a group of kids – the same kids that used to call him names – and telling them how Jesus had changed his life.

This type of work is some of the most challenging. Seeking

to bring hope in the midst of hopelessness is a tall order for anyone. As a member of a management committee for such a project I, like the others, found it difficult to assess how the work was going and whether the established aims for the project were being met. Trust in the worker was very important. When accounting for time we found it helpful for the worker to keep a journal of what he did and when. Where money is tied up with detached projects, workers have been under increasing pressure to produce 'results'. But the value of building relationships is hard to quantify and it is difficult to know what will come of them. We must be careful not to place pounds and pence before people. Recently, hard nosed economic demands have made it difficult for many projects to continue, and impossible for new ones to be started.

If we are to reach every young person, detached and unstructured youth work is vital. There will always be those who fall through the net of structured and semi-structured work. It is a gospel imperative to reach out to those who find it difficult or impossible to come to us.

GET GOING! ─────────────────────────

Types of youth work

To get a full understanding of the options and opportunities available to us we need to know what can be done and where it can happen.

In the simple grid (Fig 2.1) on page 29 study the particular characteristics of each type of youth work and what are the apparent priorities, practices and programmes that each type of youth work follows.

Using the example provided now write in other examples from your own observation and experience.

Fig 2.1 **Types of youth work (I)**

CHARACTERISTICS

NAMES	STYLE (Structured semi-structured unstructured)	PRIORITIES	PRACTICES	PROGRAMMES
Boy scouts	Structured	Following scout law and promise using hand-book to train	Badge work Team work	Scout pack meeting camps special training events
School roadshow	Unstructured	Simple communi-cation of gospel in 'credible style'	Games Drama Music Talk	Once a term in each local school

*What is **my** calling?*

We have seen earlier in the chapter that there are a number of options available to us and our churches in developing a worthwhile work among young people. But which style of work is right for us and our church?

The grid (Fig 2.2) on page 30 should help you decide. On the left the vertical axis is defined by calling. At the bottom, the horizontal axis is defined by the relationship between young people and the church. The first point on the horizontal axis represents Christian young people who are committed members of the local church. The furthest point on the horizontal axis represents non-Christian marginalised young people. Obviously, we are not able to supply all the stages between these two points on the horizontal axis, but we have supplied some of the ones that are most important.

On the vertical 'calling' axis there are five possible callings. These are not exhaustive, but seek to define general areas of ministry among young people that you may relate to.

Fig 2.2 **What is *my* calling**

	Non-Christian marginalised	No known contact with any Christians or church	knows one or two Christians	comes every now and then	fully integrated into church
Pioneer					
Interventionist					
Communicator					
Carers					
Trainer					

Proximity to church and youth workers

- **Pioneer** Someone who feels called to pioneer a new youth project, a new programme, or initiate a whole new area of youth work within the local church.

- **Interventionist** Someone called to speak to the issues and problems that young people face, and that the church faces in reaching out to young people.

- **Communicator** Someone who feels called to communicate the good news of salvation to young people and bring them to the point of discipleship to Christ within the local church.

- **Carer** Someone who feels specifically called to care for the material and spiritual needs of young people so that the obstacles to personal spiritual growth are removed.

- **Trainer** Someone who feels called to train young people to become more effective disciples of Christ.

In reading these definitions, you may feel called to do all of them! However, you need to decide what you would define as your starting point. For instance, you may feel called to be a Trainer but your first calling is to Pioneer; or to be an Interventionist, but your first calling is to be a Carer.

Looking at the grid provided, try to define your calling as it is laid out there. As a Communicator of the gospel, you may feel a special calling to the homeless; or as a Pioneer, you may feel your calling is to work with the fringe membership of a local church. Tick the box that you believe defines your place.

You may discover as you think through your calling that what you are currently doing is not what you are called to do. If this is the case, you need as a matter of some importance to discuss this with others involved.

Teamwork

Having completed the grid for yourself, encourage others in your team to do the same. This will help to reveal how balanced a team it is. Probably there would need to be more than two or three different callings within the team for it to work effectively. For instance, if you are pioneering a new project, a team that includes all Pioneers and no Carers or Trainers will tend to function with only limited success.

New projects may well be able to contact young people but will not be able to keep young people unless the right gift mix is available – the right combination of callings.

In the life of almost any project from its inception to its growth to maturity, all of the callings are needed at some time or another. Pioneers, Interventionists, Communicators, Carers and Trainers all have their special emphasis.

Discuss with your team where there are any deficiencies created by particular callings not being represented on the team. If certain callings are clearly needed to augment the life of your team, the team will be able to pray towards the recruitment of a person with that particular calling. Your current team may have been used by God to get you to where you are now, but may need the addition of other people to get it to where God is calling it next.

Team research

Some teams will be deficient but they will not know why. There will be gaps within the team but it will be unclear which gaps need filling now and which can be left until later. If this is the case, observing other teams in operation and recognising where they are successful and why, will help in defining who you need to join your team to make your work more effective.

To research effectively, team members, preferably in pairs, will need to observe other teams in operation, record what is successful in what they see and what is not. The pair of workers from your team will need to ask the other team what they think are the practical and spiritual keys to their success. Finally, ask the other team to fill in the calling grid so that you can define whether the mix of callings gives any clues as to the team's success.

This will help you multiply the success you see in other work and see the practical measures that you can take by praying for and recruiting new members to your team.

As a team you may find it helpful to use material found in Romans 12, 1 Corinthians 12, and Ephesians 4 to help define all the ways in which God has equipped the church as a 'team' to complete the task he has given us.

The Bible and relationships

Each of the styles of youth work outlined so far have their own particular characteristics and strengths which make each approach useful among different age groups and backgrounds. But these strengths are quickly dissolved if the building of deep and lasting relationships is not central. Relationships are the only means we have of enabling and encouraging young people to reach maturity in their physical, emotional, social and spiritual lives.

As Christians searching for a fuller understanding of youth work, we need to do more than just assess the different approaches available. We need to use the Bible as a guide. It will give us a deeper insight into the issues involved and should help us to minimise the weaknesses and maximise the strengths of each approach. This will be important as we decide the style of youth work which best suits our gifts, our resources and the young people we are seeking to reach.

Young people

The Bible is clear about God's commitment to the young. In the Old Testament Israel was commanded to take care of the most vulnerable young people – the orphans – or face God's judgment: 'Do not take advantage of a widow or an orphan. If you do and they cry out to me, I will certainly hear their cry' (Exodus 22:22–3).

Orphans, or the fatherless, are very common today. With a third of marriages ending in divorce and one in four children born to a single parent home, many children grow up not knowing the security of living in a home where both parents are present. Of course their parents are usually alive, but their experience of vulnerability is very similar to that of an orphan whose parents have died. God is a father to these orphans: 'A father to the fatherless, a defender of widows, is God in his holy dwelling' (Psalm 68:5).

We can have confidence because we know he takes care of

these vulnerable ones and he expects his people to reflect his concern:

> When you have finished setting aside a tenth of all your pro-
> duce in the third year, the year of the tithe, you shall give it
> to the Levite, the alien, the fatherless and the widow, so that
> they may eat in your towns and be satisfied (Deuteronomy
> 26:12).

In the New Testament, James continues this theme. Making the widows and orphans a priority is the expression of faith that God the father is looking for: 'Religion that God our father accepts as pure and faultless is this: to look after orphans and widows in their distress and to keep oneself from being pol-luted by the world' (James 1:27).

This priority of taking care of the vulnerable young is seen in the ministry of Jesus as he welcomed the children, using them as examples of the kingdom: 'Jesus said, "Let the little children come to me, and do not hinder them, for the kingdom of heaven belongs to such as these" ' (Matthew 19:14).

In reinstating Peter to his position of leadership, Jesus speci-fied that Peter should first concern himself with 'the lambs': 'When they had finished eating, Jesus said to Simon Peter, "Simon son of John, do you truly love me more than these?" "Yes, Lord," he said, "you know that I love you." Jesus said, "Feed my lambs" ' (John 21:15). Some would disagree with me, but I think Jesus is specifying the most vulnerable of his flock first. Even if this does not refer exclusively to children and young people, they are surely included among 'the lambs' in his flock. There can be no doubt that the Bible makes it clear that the young are a priority for God, and so they should be a priority for his people.

How to develop relationships
Relationships are the foundation of all that we do. Does the Bible give any insight as to how relationships should be formed and maintained? Clearly there are right ways and

wrong ways to have a relationship.

Right relationships. Righteousness is one of the central themes of the Bible. It actually means 'right relationships'. Understanding righteousness in this way helps us to understand some of the key verses in the Bible. For instance, when Jesus says, 'But seek first his kingdom and his righteousness, and all these things will be given to you as well' (Matthew 6:33), he means that God's rule and the right relationships that he defines should be our first priority. God is concerned to promote and maintain right relationships, both with himself and among his people, at all costs – even at the cost of his Son. Jesus described the right relationship that should exist in the kingdom between one person and another in terms of service. To be a servant in the kingdom is to be righteous. But when Jesus is talking about servants and service, what exactly does he mean?

> Jesus said to them, 'The kings of the Gentiles lord it over them; and those who exercise authority over them call themselves benefactors. But you are not to be like that. Instead, the greatest among you should be like the youngest, and the one who rules like the one who serves' (Luke 22:25–6).

Jesus says both what servants are and what they are not. Servants are not those with power and authority. They are not the benefactors. Servants are the least, the lowest rank, at the bottom of the pile.

Servant relationships. The problem for most of us is not that we do not recognise the need to serve, but that our model of service is not a biblical one. For instance, when service is used in expressions like 'education service', 'civil service' and even 'religious service', we mean that certain resources are made available or provided and that those who are the 'servants' deliver the goods. For many Christians, servants are those who have something to give from their own resources. This means that Christians often describe service as giving surplus time, energy and money to benefit others.

Unfortunately this is the opposite of what Jesus means by service. He specifically says that servants are not to be benefactors (Luke 22:25–6). Benefactors usually create relationships of dependency in those to whom they give. This causes problems for both the giver and receiver. The givers easily forget that they are the recipients of God's grace, that they have nothing of value other than what God has given and that in fact their lives are bankrupt and of no use to anyone, least of all God, unless he chooses to use them and puts something worthwhile within them. The recipients easily lose focus on God as the giver, and can quickly begin to duck the responsibility of seeking him for their daily bread. A provider-client relationship has been created.

Although giving from our resources is something which God expects from his people, the basis of Christian service is something altogether more radical. Service is more than giving from our resources; it is giving our lives. A servant could do nothing else in the time of Jesus because they were nobodies who owned nothing.

> Suppose one of you had a servant ploughing or looking after the sheep. Would he say to the servant when he comes in from the field, 'Come along now and sit down to eat'? Would he not rather say, 'Prepare my supper, get yourself ready and wait on me while I eat and drink; after that you may eat and drink'? Would he thank the servant because he did what he was told to do? So you also, when you have done everything you were told to do, should say, 'We are unworthy servants; we have only done our duty' (Luke 17:7–10).

Being a servant is not making available what you feel you can manage to give, but realising you have nothing, and that God must first give to you before you can pass it on. We may find it offensive that we should consider ourselves to count for so little, but this kingdom value system is there for a reason. It is only when we focus on God's value system that everything else falls into place. His value on our lives is the one that matters and he places the highest price – the life of his Son – on our heads. This value, given to us by him, counts for so much that everything else should count for nothing. This was something Paul knew particularly well:

> But whatever was to my profit I now consider loss for the sake of Christ. What is more, I consider everything a loss compared to the surpassing greatness of knowing Christ Jesus my Lord, for whose sake I have lost all things. I consider them rubbish, that I may gain Christ, and be found in him, not having a righteousness of my own that comes from the law, but that which is through faith in Christ – the righteousness that comes from God and is by faith (Philippians 3:7–9).

Having already reflected upon the service and sacrifice of Jesus in the second chapter of Philippians, Paul shows us how to apply the same principles to our lives. When we realise that Jesus gave up everything (Philippians 2:5–11) that was his by right to win a relationship with us, we are prepared to give up all our rights for him. We should be like him and consider ourselves to be nothing to that what is of real value – God's love and life – can come through. If we are servants we cannot be providers. Only God provides. This may seem a small point, but it accounts for a great deal of failure if we don't get it right.

Provider-client relationships. All too often we feel that our role is to 'put something on' for young people, creating a provider-client relationship. In the end this type of relationship helps no one. The providers (youth workers, pastors etc) feel burdened by the full weight of putting on a programme of interest to attract the clients (young people). The clients feel uninvolved, uninformed and uninterested. Faced by this the providers redouble their efforts, but of course to no end. This situation is exacerbated when Christian youth workers believe they are doing the right thing because they are 'serving' the young people.

If we are to be biblical, then serving young people should not be about putting on a programme to attract interest or entice. We should be the opposite of providers. When Jesus sent his disciples out to proclaim the kingdom he did not ask them to provide anything for those they sought to reach, but rather expected that those being reached would be the providers (Luke 9:4, 10:8). How to apply this idea in creating a programme will be looked at more deeply in a later chapter. Not being a provider is a vital understanding that for many youth workers will require a complete change of mind and approach.

Whether our experience is in a uniformed organisation or in other kinds of structured youth work, in a youth club or on the streets in detached work, it is vital that we do not create a provider-client relationship. This relationship is not based on a biblical understanding of service and because of this is 'unrighteous' – an unright relationship. If the right relationships are not established we find anxiety is created and we become weighed down with responsibility. But if the right relationships are established at the outset, we have peace and we can point to Jesus as the burden carrier:

> Come to me, all you who are weary and burdened, and I will give you rest. Take my yoke upon you and learn from me, for I am gentle and humble in heart, and you will find rest for your souls. For my yoke is easy and my burden is light (Matthew 11:28–30).

At All Saints Brixton Hill we sought to develop a youth project reaching young people from five to eighteen years which is based on non provider-client relationships. The children and young people we work with participate at every level in creating the programmes that we run. Our experience is that although there needs to be a different application for different ages, it is nevertheless possible to do. More importantly, when we do it this way many of the pressures are related and the project is more successful in every way.

GET GOING!

Having seen the options available and the ways in which we might get involved, it is important to ensure that we understand the strengths and weaknesses of the type of work we are called to, and particularly the potential within this kind of work to develop provider-client relationships. Being aware of these things will enable us to look for others to develop other work in our area to meet the needs of the young people that we will not reach and help us to prevent the slide into the problems caused by the provider-client relationships.

The grid below is similar to the 'Types of youth work' grid on page 29, except that we now have strengths, weaknesses and a rating that indicates the strength of the tendency towards the provider-client relationship. By this we mean that if a particular type of work has a strong tendency towards developing provider client relationships it will have a rating of 8, 9 or 10. If it has a small tendency it will have a rating of 1, 2 or 3. Again, examples will be given and the rest will be left to you and your own judgment.

Fig 2.3 **Types of youth work (II)**

CHARACTERISTICS

NAMES	STYLE (Structured semi-structured unstructured)	STRENGTHS	WEAKNESSES	PROVIDER CLIENT TENDENCY (1–10)
Boy scouts	Structured	Discipline Team work Strong moral code	Being activity based the relationships can be overlooked	7–8
School roadshow	Unstructured	Contact many young people	Difficult to form and maintain relationships	9–10

It would perhaps be good to do this exercise with others so as to ensure that you get as balanced and complete a view of the different types of work as possible. For instance, you may be particularly aware of the weaknesses of one style of work, but unaware of its strengths, whereas another may be able to list its strengths, but unable to see its weaknesses.

Conclusion

Whatever style or approach to youth work we are called into, relationships are always the key to success. But the 'right relationship' is one of service. True servants never create provider client relationships because they realise they have nothing to provide – only lives to lay down. God is the king and he has shown us the way by laying down his life for us. He is our only provider. Our great joy is that we know him and he has promised that as we seek his kingdom and his right relationships, he will provide.

Developing a total approach

The problem of decline

Every church leader and youth worker knows the pain of losing young people. People who were once active, sincere young Christians now seem to live in a spiritual wilderness, far away from God and unconnected to any church.

The English Church Census provides indisputable evidence that the church is very poor at keeping young people and in reaching young people who are not Christians. The census figures show that over the last ten years the church has lost about 900 children, teenagers and young adults per week, roughly 300 children under fifteen, 400 between fifteen and nineteen years and 200 between twenty and twenty-nine years. These staggering figures show that children's work and work among young people has been largely unsuccessful over the past decade.

Even the losses among young adults (those between twenty and twenty-nine years old) are affected by poor youth work. If the church had adequate methods of evangelism and Christian nurture, we would not lose so many. Churches often see a considerable drop in commitment among young people as they go to college or university or start full time employment. Even if a college has a strong and committed Christian presence the drop off rate after college is enormous. One Christian Union executive member told me that his research had revealed that of all previous Christian Union presidents and executive members at his college, only one third were now committed members of a local church.

Although the drop in attendance among children, recorded in the census figures, is not as drastic in percentage terms as that among teenagers and young adults, it is still a cause for concern. Nationally the birth rate has dropped over the past few years and so it would be expected that fewer children would be going to church. Although we should take some comfort from the fact that the church seems to be almost 'holding its own' among children, the figures still represent decline, and not growth. (See *Christian England* by Peter Brierley [MARC Europe 1991] pp 81–2.)

There are specific reasons why the church has traditionally been good at children's work, and continues, to some extent, to attract large numbers of children. There are also reasons why, since the war, these children have not been kept within the body of the local church.

I would suggest that the main cause of the phenomenal decline among teenagers and young adults is that the church does not use the appropriate methods to reach and keep young people. Our methods and approach is adequate only so far as it is applied to children. But even here there is no room for complacency. Our methods appear only to work well among girls. The figures show that many more girls than boys go to church.

Christian parents and grandparents take their children along to church. But as soon as the children are able, or allowed to choose for themselves, they stop coming along. Where this is not the case and children are successfully engaged and interested by well run children's programmes, they are lost as soon as they are expected to move up from the children's programme to the programme laid on for teenagers. What are the reasons for this?

Provider-client relationships: the problem re-examined

When a child is born, it is totally dependent upon its parents for food, warmth and protection. This relationship of dependency continues through childhood. Although children of six and seven are not as dependent as new born babies, they still need their parents to feed, clothe and protect them. Intimate relationships of care and trust with parents and other adults at this stage provide a secure foundation for a balanced growth towards adulthood and maturity.

Often children do not receive the levels of love, care and attention at home that they need to grow up healthily. When this is the case the inner need for these things does not disappear but remains with the child. To meet these needs, a child will accept love from other adults such as teachers, Sunday school workers, and the like. Even where a child is growing up in a healthy home environment, other adults are needed to show love and concern. Teachers of the youngest age groups in infant schools find that hugs, physical touch and expressions of care are needed to help the child adjust to school life.

All of this is fertile ground for the provider-client relationship to grow. However, if children's work develops around the provider-client relationship eventually problems will surface, even though at the outset everything seems fine. Childhood dependency means that children need adults to provide certain things, and the church, having swallowed the provider-client relationship hook, line and sinker, is able to function quite well in this context. As soon as young people desire independence, wishing to take their place in the world as non-dependent adults, the approach does not work. A different approach is needed.

If we operate from the perspective of biblical service introduced in chapter two, it is possible to avoid these problems. Biblical service is sacrifice which flexibly responds to each new situation. If service can only be given when people are dependent, we have to ask whether it really is sacrificial at all. Sacrifice by its very nature is applicable to every person in every situation. For it to be true sacrifice it must be related to those whom we serve.

For a child, we act sacrificially when we give time, energy and money to meet their need for loving adult input which we ask God to provide through the people of the church. For a teenager, serving them will mean something different. It will involve helping them to think for themselves, explore the world and their response to it, and giving them the opportunity to develop good judgment through personal choice. For an adult it will mean making the assumption that they are able to function as one among equals, able to choose to change their lives and the way they affect others. Here are two examples.

Summer Playscheme

Our Summer Playscheme, held every year during the school holidays for junior school kids, is now created around the ideas of the children themselves. The young people are placed into small groups of similar ages with two or three leaders. Their first task is to create a two week programme for themselves. A budget is given to the group from grants received to run the Playscheme, and the group is expected, with guidance, to use it wisely.

The groups have consistently produced interesting and creative programmes for themselves. Everything from sight-seeing to safari parks, swimming to video making have been tried. The only other things included in the programme are one or two joint trips which they are encouraged to participate in and a suggestion that one day is given for some kind of community service, again of their own choice. Help and guidance in creating a balanced programme is given by the leaders, which is entirely appropriate given that we are working with children. But because we are wanting to avoid a provider-client type of programme the children are much more involved in what goes on.

This approach has been remarkably successful, much more successful than previous attempts at playschemes which we simply laid on. Gone are the days of rushing around months before the playscheme trying to mount an attractive programme and raising the funds to run it. Today we spend our efforts in building relationships and overseeing and encouraging the young people as they mount their own programmes.

Talking to youth workers, the greatest advantage of not developing provider-client relationships is the 'stress factor'.

If the young people are largely responsible for their own programme, the burden of this responsibility for their success
need not be carried by the workers themselves. Also, attracting
and maintaining membership becomes less of a factor because
the young people are more likely to commit themselves to a
programme they have created than one they have been given.
Our experience is that low attendance is hardly ever a problem. The Playscheme is always over-subscribed. No longer do
we wonder from day to day whether they will turn up for a
particular part of the programme; the problem never arises!

Family relationships

In the last few years we have had two new members added to
the Breen family. One was Samuel, born in 1990, the other
was Michelle, who in 1989, at the age of fourteen, joined our
family. She was excited recently to discover that her name
has now been changed from her original family name to Breen
on her official documents.

Sally (my wife) and I would be the first to admit many
mistakes have been made. Helping Michelle overcome her
difficult, and at times tragic, past has meant loving her by
helping her to take responsibility for her new life and her new
future. Because of her past, Michelle was a prime candidate
for developing a dependency relationship with me and Sally
from which she might never have escaped. Our task as parents,
as with all our other children, was to see her grow to maturity,
free from unhelpful dependency relationships.

This transition has at times been difficult, painful, even
stormy, but now as Michelle takes her place as an adult
member of the local community and the local church, it all
seems worthwhile. Not developing dependency or provider-
client relationships is a fight worth fighting.

The graph below is my personal observation of how, typi-
cally, people develop in their level of independence against
time. The 'dip' records the struggle which most young people
go through. They want to be dependent, 'looked after' by some-

one and may develop co-dependent relationships with other young people or adults. These co-dependent relationships are fertile ground for provider-client relationships. Once free of these relationships, young people will quickly assert their independence, as shown on the graph.

Fig 3.1   Dependency Against Time for Child Members of Church

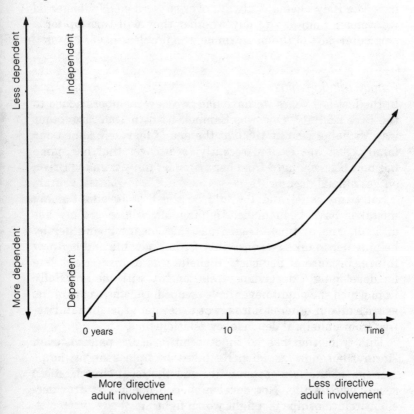

Of course, children, teenagers and adults may, as individuals, be at all sorts of different stages of development, with all sorts of different needs. Some adults will have reached physical maturity without the accompanying growth to intellectual and

emotional maturity. But this only means that our approach needs to be more flexible.

The aim of Christian service is to equip others to serve (Ephesians 4:11–13), which leads to Christian maturity. The inbuilt, though largely unexpressed aim of the provider-client relationship is continuous dependency, meaning that Christians always remain as vulnerable infants in the Christian life (Ephesians 4:14).

If we are to remove the provider-client relationship as the single most important influence in Christian ministry and outreach we must have our minds changed. It is our Western, secular mindset which for years has told us that service always equals provision, that needs to change. The problem is that it is so ingrained that nothing less than a revolution in our thinking will suffice. Its power is nothing short of demonic and represents a stronghold in the mind of which Paul speaks in 2 Corinthians 10:4–6.

The clergy one-man-band syndrome, or the elders' four (five, six, seven . . .)-man-band, so pervasive in the British church, is another expression of this problem. We perceive our leaders as providers rather than servants, and the body of Christ as dependent clients, receiving what is dished out rather than taking responsibility for mature Christian service. Whenever this approach is in place we can expect that evangelism among teenagers and young adults will be patchy, if not non-existent. Commitment levels among the senior adult membership of the church will also be affected, because provider-client relationships by their very nature keep people dependent and immature. Maturity is only possible when people are encouraged to take responsibility for being a Christian and serving others.

If the problems created by the provider-client relationship are addressed, then much of the inertia which prevents mission and growth will be removed from the body of Christ. For this to take place, provider-client relationships must be removed from every level of the church's life. To do this requires a 'total' or 'holistic' approach. Seeing the church and all its work as a single organism, bearing witness to the king-

dom in different ways to different people at different stages of
their life is surely the right way to look at the body of Christ.
Youth work, along with children's work and work among
young adults can then be integrated with the whole life of the
church. It can also be overseen by leaders concerned for the
whole body. Unfortunately this is not always the case.

Fig 3.2   Dependency Against Time for Adult Converts

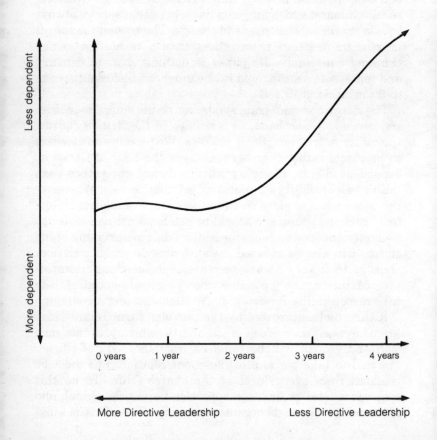

Fig 3.2 on page 48 represents my own observation of an adult's dependency against time since becoming a Christian. As with children, new Christians go through a 'dip' where they apparently stop growing in Christian maturity and want to be dependent on others for their spiritual imput. This is the 'danger zone' for developing a long term provider-client relationship. Leaders beware!

Now the young people will sing to us!

Churches may take pride in their youth programmes, but still see them as an adjunct to the main 'adult' programmes of the church. How many times have the adult leaders and members thought they were encouraging their young people by giving them the opportunity to 'do their thing' as part of the weekly service? The adults smile, nod and murmur with approval as the young people 'perform', then go and continue to spend most of their time, money and energy on maintaining the adult programme in the church.

Out of the 1,000 or so people lost to the church each week, 900 are under twenty-nine. This should mean that nine tenths of our resources in evanglism should be spent on children and young people.

Some churches do in fact spend a considerable amount on their children's and youth programmes. But even when these resources are spent it is often for the wrong reasons. So often the children's and youth work programmes in the church are there primarily to appease and encouarge anxious parents. The parents are fearful that their children will be unfulfilled and leave the church, and so apply pressure to the leadership to spend the church's resources on meeting their needs. This means that the church's resources are largely spent on ourselves rather than on those who are lost.

I overheard a minister discussing with his children's worker what they should do about the trouble caused by young people from outside the church fellowship joining the church's programmes and disrupting the activities. He told the children's

worker to ban the disruptive kids and concentrate his effort
on the children of church families. His reasons were that if
this was not done, they were liable to lose the children –
including the church kids.

At first this reasoning seems fine, but when you consider
the message given to all those affected by it, you have to doubt
its wisdom. The non church kids were told that they were
unwanted, and the church parents and children were allowed
to continue with the impression that they did not need to take
responsibility for their unconverted peers. I doubt that those
church children would have had much chance of growing into
mature active witnesses of Christ if such a policy was continued.

The clear though undeclared objective of many children's
and youth programmes is to keep the adults in the church
happy, 'giving' members and to ensure that their children keep
coming along. This is not a kingdom principle. Giving of our
resources to ensure that the children or Christian families are
nurtured to maturity in the faith is good and right, but if this
is done simply to please the parents it is undoubtedly wrong.
If it results in keeping unconverted young people away, it is
a tragedy. It will mean that the kingdom of God, based as it
is on sacrificial service, will not be advanced. It will also inevitably mean that inappropriate styles of work develop.

The provider-client relationship invariably leads to patronising attitudes. Young people see what is going on, rebel and
leave. These patronising attitudes are not usually conscious,
but are based on a misunderstanding of Christian service, a
lack of awareness of kingdom priorities and the anxieties of
parents for their children 'in the world'.

When the decision is made by a church to spend a significant
proportion of their human and financial resources on youth
work it should be for the right reasons. The resources need to
be for the benefit of young people and the style of work needs
to be effective in both keeping those who are already Christians and reaching those that are not. If we don't spend our
resources in this sacrificial way there is little chance of us

reaching and keeping young people. When resources are spent we should follow the kingdom principles of receiving through giving. Adults will need to be prepared to sacrifice some of their anxieties as well as their time and money to produce the right programmes to reach those outside the church.

For this to work it must be taken on in a way that touches everyone. A total approach is necessary. This means developing an integrated approach across the church using the church's resources in manpower and money. The church leaders and youth workers need to work together to ensure that work done among young people has a connection with all the other work done in and through the church.

From the youth worker's point of view this means developing a 'flow' from children's work through youth work to the work done among young adults. From the church leader's point of view it means helping the youth workers see beyond their own 'patch' to take in the whole body of Christ. Youth workers and leaders need to ensure that there are no 'watertight compartments' in which one area of work is done to the exclusion of all others. This may seem radical, and it may be that you do not feel ready for such an approach. But the situation is serious and requires nothing short of a radical solution.

GET GOING! ─────────────────────

To develop an overall approach to youth work which is able to maintain a twin focus of reaching and keeping young people, it must be integrated into everything else that is going on. This requires a strategy.

Strategy and vision
A strategy is by its very nature inclusive and encompassing. It begins with vision. We need to ask ourselves what God has called us into existence to do. The question has both a general and specific application.

The universal church of Jesus Christ has been called into existence to do certain things. For instance to worship God, to live in unity and to witness to the good news of salvation. But these need to be applied specifically to every local situation. Each church is called to have a witness and a work within a specific community or among a particular group of people. This will dictate the particular things that we do. is a grid which I call 'the frozen p's', which is loosely based on John Wimber's *Writing Your History in Advance* tape series. The grid is a way of recording and planning an inclusive strategy for you and your church.

To begin, fill out the grid as an *individual*, asking other workers and leaders to do the same. Then together *collectively* fill in a grid for the whole church.

(a) **Parameters**. These are the boundaries of our ministry, both individual and corporate. The parameters of our ministry are defined by our calling – what we believe God wants us to do – and by the way God equips us by his Spirit to fulfil our calling. I have tried to show how I would write down my own series of 'frozen p's' as they relate to just one parameter. In the example I have used, my parameter is a *calling* to reach young people with the gospel of the kingdom through the gift of evangelism. This is one part of my own calling and gifting but perhaps your parameters would not include either of these. What is certain is that we all have more than one parameter that we must work to.

For me other parameters that would come even before a calling to evangelism among young people would be my personal calling to follow Jesus, my calling to be a loving husband to my wife and my calling to be a good father to my children. These kind of parameters need to be filled in first because the priorities, practices and programmes that follow these will define the time and energy available for our other areas of calling.

(b) Priorities. Our parameters will undergird our priorities. Priorities need to be listed not according to how you think other people will want you to put them but by what you believe your priorities ought to be. Having listed them, be ready to talk them through with someone else. If at this stage you need to change them, then do, but first put down your own ideas. See the example for how I would express *my* priorities based on the parameter of evangelism. Would you put it differently?

(c) Practices. Our priorities will lead to a definition of expected practices for ourselves and for the members of our church.

For instance, the priority of fellowship will be revealed in the practice of small groups. The programme which comes next will be defined by structure – what you do in them and how you operate in small groups. 'Plant' will identify where the group meeting takes place.

(d) Programmes. Programmes are created by finding a structure by which we can organise our basic practices. Programmes will come and go as we learn new ways of expressing our priorities through our basic Christian practices.

For instance, in an attempt not to create provider-client relationships, All Saints Youth Project has a priority of friendship evangelism which is expressed in the practice of meeting in small groups. What those groups do and how they function will change from time to time as God leads us into new things.

(e) Personnel. People are needed to run programmes. If this is to be done successfully they need to be trained, equipped and released to do it. Programmes are only ever successful if people are available to mount and maintain them. Those who are released to run programmes in this way need to know that the programme may not last forever. As new ways of expressing practices are found, new programmes, and therefore different training, and sometimes different people are needed.

Fig 3.3 **The Frozen P's**

PARAMETERS	PRIORITIES	PRACTICES	PROGRAMMES	PERSONNEL
Evangelism: A *calling* to reach young people with the gospel of the kingdom through the gift of evangelism	a Meeting people on equal terms b Natural witness to what God has done for *me* c Presentation of Gospel d Boldness to call others to repentance and faith	a Make friends of non Christians b Pray for new friends c Pray for boldness	Small groups – A-Teams Socialise regularly with new friends	One other partner in evangelism
PLANT	POUNDS & PENCE	PLANNING		PRAYER
None needed unless want to meet at home. Otherwise meet in 'community facilities' (ie pub)	Money to buy tracts (short explanation of the Gospel) Perhaps buy a Bible and Bible notes for when converted	a Find a partner b Identify a person to evangelise c Make friends d Set up socialising programme e Share faith f Conversion repentance & faith g Buy Bible and notes h Set up membership of small group for initial follow-up and nurture i Church and attendance	One month indefinite amount of time One month	– pray for right person – pray for friendship – pray for opportunity – pray for growth – pray for settling in to group – pray for settling in to church

(f) Plant. The use of buildings should reflect our programmes and the needs of our personnel to run the programmes. Buildings that only reflect one set of priorities (eg worship) are very common, and often useless for most of our other programmes.

(g) Pounds and pence. Our parameters, priorities, practices, programmes, personnel and plant need to be priced up, planned for and prayed over! (Try saying that without your teeth in!) The cost of a programme should be recognised from the beginning so that we are not caught out later on in the programme with no money to meet the financial needs. This does not represent a lack of faith, just stewardship of God's resources and good sense.

(h) Planning. Making a plan is a relatively simple task of organising our programmes over a defined time period. Overall planning should begin with the longest amount of time we can visualise. At first this may not be very far – perhaps only a couple of months – but with practice this should increase to two, three, four or even five years!

Bad planning puts all the effort into the immediate future and forgets about the long term view. Good planning puts all the effort into the long term and lets tomorrow take care of itself. (See Fig 3.4 on page 56).

(i) Prayer. Prayer must undergird all that we do, not because we hope that God will somehow come in and 'back up our act', but because we are dependent on him for everything. It is his kingdom, his calling, his work, his people, his resources, his plan and ultimately his glory we are seeking to reflect.

Fig 3.4   Good and Bad Planning

BAD PLANNING
Spending most of our planning time on tomorrow and hardly any on next year!

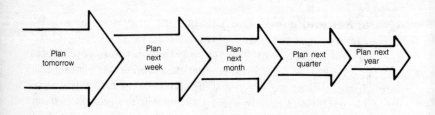

GOOD PLANNING

Spending most of our planning time on the long term and letting tomorrow's plans be dictated by the *plans* for the future not the *reactions* of today!

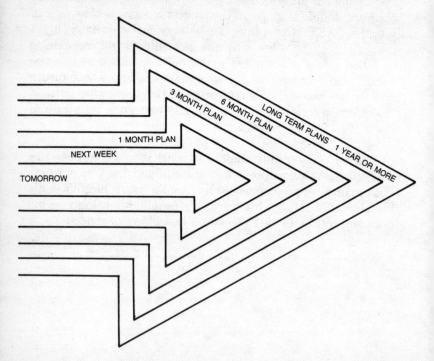

Repentance and faith

To make the changes spoken about in the first two chapters means taking a big step.

Chapter one spoke about reaching out from one culture to another, requiring an ability to understand the world from another person's perspective. Chapters two and three spoke of removing provider-client relationships from our work, involving a radical reappraisal of all we do in the light of the Bible's teaching on service. At the heart of both chapters is an emphasis on relationships as the key to all we do. Implementing these things means making fundamental changes to the way we think and act.

If we are able to see the world from the perspective of God the king, and if we are able to understand the world in the terms of his rule, change becomes part of being in the kingdom. It is impossible to enter the kingdom without change first taking place in our lives. Jesus made this clear as he came proclaiming the nearness of God's rule: 'Jesus went into Galilee, proclaiming the good news of God. "The time has come," he said. "The kingdom of God is near. Repent and believe the good news!" ' (Mark 14:1).

But repentance and belief are not isolated events that only take place as we come to the king and enter his kingdom. They are part of a process which begins when we first respond to the good news and which continues as we remain in the kingdom. (See Fig 4.1 on page 58.)

The word that the New Testament writers most often used for repentance was 'metanoia'. This means to have your mind changed. Having our mind changed means that our actions can follow suit.

Metanoia was always intended to be a continuous process of

change so that our whole way of seeing, understanding, and believing is transformed by the work of God in our lives. As this change takes place, we are able to obey God as we put into practice by faith what he calls us to do. For this reason, repentance and faith should always be thought of as two parts of a single process.

Fig 4.1   The repentance loop (I)

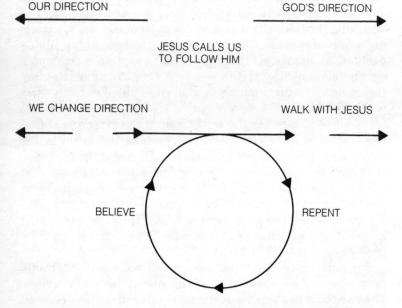

When we repent and believe we turn around and change the way we think and act. Jesus, as he proclaimed the good news of the kingdom called people to do just that, turn around and change – but he expected the process to continue. We need to change direction to enter the kingdom, and this will mean going through the experience of repentance and faith. Notice in the diagram that repentance involves looking at the direction we were going in (the things we did, said and thought) and then making a decision to go in a new direction in the belief that we will be sustained as we go.

The story of the prodigal son reveals this important truth. For repentence and change to take place the boy needed to face reality. In a far off country, having lost everything, he comes to the point of repentance. Literally he saw himself for what he was:

> When he came to his senses, he said, 'How many of my father's hired men have food to spare, and here I am starving to death! I will set out and go back to my father and say to him: Father, I have sinned against heaven and against you. I am no longer worthy to be called your son; make me like one of your hired men.' So he got up and went to his father (Luke 15:17–20).

On his return the son was restored and forgiven and the slate was wiped clean. When speaking to his older son who found it more difficult to forgive, the father said, 'This brother of yours was dead and is alive again; he was lost and is found' (Luke 15:32).

Forgiveness, both seeking it and giving it, are constant themes in the teaching of Jesus. Forgiveness is one way of continuing the process of repentance and belief. When we seek forgiveness from God (or from anyone else) we turn away from – repent of – our sin and believe it has then been dealt with by our heavenly Father. When we give forgiveness we help others to repent and believe that God will restore them.

To experience forgiveness means going through the same process of repentance and belief. To repent means to look at what we did that was wrong, confess it to God and decide in faith to go in a new direction, believing we are forgiven.

Forgiveness in human relationships works in the same way as forgiveness in our relationship with God. (See Fig 4.2 on page 60.)

Looking at what we have done requires a discipline which we often find difficult. We need someone to help us with this discipline. My experience of youth work is that Jesus constantly challenges, encourages and helps us to repent and believe. As we respond, he is able to help us change the way we see and do things and make our youth work reflect more of his kingdom.

Fig 4.2   The repentance loop (II)

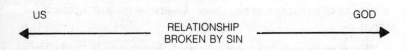
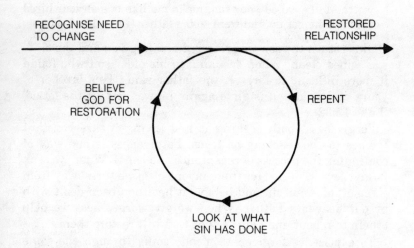

US   GOD
                        RELATIONSHIP
                        BROKEN BY SIN

RECOGNISE NEED   RESTORED
TO CHANGE   RELATIONSHIP

BELIEVE
GOD FOR   REPENT
RESTORATION

LOOK AT WHAT
SIN HAS DONE

Repentance at the Romsey Mill

During my time as Team Leader of the Romsey Mill Youth and Community Centre in Cambridge, I began to realise that the Lord was calling us to change. I had a feeling that the change was going to be radical.

I had become dissatisfied and somewhat disillusioned by the clubs which we ran throughout the week at different times and for different ages. Some productive work was being done, but we never seemed to achieve what we were looking for. We wanted to develop deep relationships with the young people who came, we wanted to see them grow up and mature, and most of all we wanted to see them become disciples of Jesus.

Although all of this was happening to a degree, there was so much more that seemed necessary. The clubs themselves were a difficult environment in which to build relationships. Often we found ourselves supervising activities or policing the building. Many of the younger members found it difficult to integrate and they were intimidated by the presence of the fifth year boys. Having reached the age of sixteen and their final year of club membership, these boys represented the real power in the club. Without their help and approval club nights could be extremely difficult. Without our intervention the girls hardly got a look in on the equipment or in the gym – the older boys were totally dominant and the younger boys were afraid to challenge their position. Of course we tried to address this problem in a number of ways, but the pattern had been set. Only something fundamental was going to change it.

Some nights were more stressful than others, but the fun and the fulfilment seemed to be going out of it. Many of the programme ideas and special events that we tried were flops. We would sometimes catch ourselves trying to be positive, finding something good to say about what was going on. But in our hearts we knew things could not continue the way they were.

I now realise God was allowing this situation to develop to create a context in which repentance and change could take place. God was calling us to repent. We began by looking at spending more time with people and less time policing, but this required more staff, and struggle as we might, no one came forward.

We tried sharing decisions and power with the young people, setting up a youth committee, but after a faltering start it eventually gave up the ghost and died. We tried a junior leader scheme where teenagers were invited to help with the children's club, this was more successful than the other ideas.

But it required a lot of input as we tried to lay on training for the new workers. Involvement in the clubs was fine, training was more difficult. It was hard to get the level right. When I asked one of the leaders what they thought about the session, she said, 'I don't know, I didn't understand most of it and so I went to sleep!'

More by way of chance than design, we had started two small groups which met outside of the normal club programme. One was a group of boys who wanted to spend time together because they were all friends. The other was a group of girls who wanted to do a project together setting up their own fashion show. As we worked with these groups and talked about the problems we were facing, we realised that much of what we were looking for in the clubs was already happening in these two small groups. In time, we used them as pilot groups to test our ideas and to try new things. Even though these groups seemed to be very successful, the rest of the work seemed to be falling apart at the seams.

Often when others are faced with similar problems, God is calling them to make changes within their current structure. In this case I knew he was calling us to a complete change. To learn what God was trying to teach us would require a wholesale turnaround. But this would involve big decisions and the management committee would have to agree. Some of us decided to fast and pray to ask God for direction. We could have improved a number of things; the training sessions could have been done better, but in the end we came to a common mind. The clubs would have to close.

Anything short of this would have been inadequate, like moving around the furniture when God wanted to rebuild the house. We later realised that God wanted to kill off the pro-vider-client mentality once and for all. To do this required a radical change, which for others may not need to be so fundamental. For us it was because without such a radical change we would have never fully implemented the message God was trying to get across.

We were quite clear about what God was saying – the teenage club, which met on Tuesdays and Thursdays, would stop at the end of the academic year, so we spent the summer term and summer holidays making plans for September when the school year began. There was little opposition to these plans from the club members, except for the fifteen year old boys who were losing the prospect of becoming senior members and of being the masters of all they surveyed!

The alternative to clubs and the new approach to youth work at the Mill came from an unexpected quarter. I had read about the base communities in Latin America. I could see the way that God was blessing these communities made up of the most poor and vulnerable of Latin American society, and I knew that here was a revelation of God's presence and power which I had not seen. Perhaps God wanted us to use small groups of some kind.

Certainly small groups seemed to be central to what God was doing among his people all around the world from Latin America to China, Africa to Korea. But in the Western church small groups had been largely restricted to Christians and the activities had been diluted to Bible study and cups of coffee. The small groups we were looking for were non religious, active and relationship based, an environment where youth workers could work alongside young people, befriend them and share their faith. We had two running models of what we were looking for, in the small boys' group and the girls' fashion group, which had now been meeting for almost a year.

We decided to work with the local secondary school and launch the groups through the first, second and third year tutorial system. We called them Alpha groups and publicised them using the idea that the members could decide their own programme. We would work with them to help fulfil their dreams. The response was completely overwhelming. We had three times as many young people sign up for groups as we expected, and from that day to this, low membership or lack of interest has not been a problem.

Alpha groups at the Romsey Mill

Each group had between six and twelve members and the membership of the group was entirely voluntary and in the hands of the group itself. This meant the group was based on existing and established relationships – peer groups. Each Alpha group developed their own programme. Some did pretty much the same thing every week, for instance there was a five a side football group and a basketball group. Others developed interesting and varied programmes covering a number of different activities.

Most groups used the facilities of the Romsey Mill, which included a gym, games room, lounge and coffee bar; some also used the school sports facilities. This meant that the investment in buildings and equipment made over the years was not wasted. In fact, more young people used the facilities than ever before.

Each group was encouraged to negotiate for time and facilities at the Mill, so that more than one group could use the place at a time. One group would use the gym whilst another used the games room. But there was no signing in and signing out at the front door and no formal club times and the building was used when the groups wanted to use it.

For the youth workers this new approach was both unsettling and liberating. With the Tuesday and Thursday clubs now out of the way it felt like our weekly anchor points had been lost. For a while we felt vulnerable and a bit lacking in confidence. But we soon saw that the benefits which liberated our time and talents outweighed any initial lack of confidence we might feel.

Youth workers were now in pairs working with one group at a time, so no policing of the facilities was necessary. We could spend all our time concentrating on the work in hand. Because the pressure to create a programme had now gone and was in the hands of the young people our efforts could be concentrated on building relationships. Unwittingly we had broken the provider-client relationship and the results we hoped for in our work began to be realised more and more.

Relationships deepened between workers and young people. Growth to maturity was encouraged more effectively and young people became Christians.

Brixton

When a couple of years later I became vicar of All Saints Brixton Hill and moved with my family and a team of people to Brixton, we took this approach to youth work with us. We continued to develop the ideas we had begun in Cambridge and renamed the groups 'A-Teams'.

Here we had no equipment, no youth club building, only a small new church building that provided two large rooms, one where the church met to worship and an adjoining hall. However, with the experience of Alpha groups under our belt we knew that facilities were great if you had them, but unnecessary if you didn't. Forming a group, encouraging it to create a programme and building relationships was what counted. So we went to work, setting up A-Teams, first with the contacts the church already had, and then beyond. Groups were usually formed by identifying one young person, befriending them and getting time to introduce us to their group of friends. The group was introduced to the idea of A-Teams and encouraged to think up a programme.

As each group tried to come up with their own programme they were encouraged to brainstorm as many ideas as possible. Sometimes the group needed to be encouraged to look beyond their current experience to new things that they might do. Living in a city means having the benefit of many different leisure activities which could easily be included in a programme. Once all the ideas had been tabled, the group produced a six week programme by voting for their favourite things. At the end of the six weeks everything was reviewed.

Many groups went away for weekends or even longer, strengthening the relationships within the group. Every so often more than one group would meet up for a shared activity, perhaps a trip to the seaside, and once a year the groups were encouraged to join together for a residential weekend away.

We also had 'secondary level events' designed to maintain contact between the groups. Secondary level events were an opportunity for more than one group to share a programme event. This could be simply done by suggesting that two groups who had the same idea for a programme, eg swimming, could do it together. Occasionally, perhaps once a term, we would organise a trip to which all the teams were invited. This would be an idea which came from one of the teams, eg dry slope skiing, that would be fun for everyone.

Much of our experience in setting up A-Teams was similar to that for Alpha groups, but there were some differences and developments. The groups were often smaller and more intimate. We put this down to the fact that an inner city environment demands more of a young person and so peer groups, which are established earlier, are smaller and more closely knit, partly for self preservation. This meant that A-Teams often included younger people than we had encountered before. Groups of teenagers would include members who were ten to eleven years old. We found that because peer groups were established earlier, A-Teams could be started in the final year of junior school.

And all this began with the process of repentance and faith.

GET GOING!

We need to allow the process of repentance and faith to be deep, continuous and long lasting. It is here that the 'learning loop' can play a useful part. I have found that having a discipline of working through the loop on a regular basis is vital. The same process outlined in chapter one for understanding others can be used for ourselves and our work. (See Fig 4.3 on page 67.)

Perhaps a summary of our experience of discovering and implementing A-Teams at the Romsey Mill Youth and Community Centre, written in terms of the six stages of the learning loop, will help you write your own.

Fig 4.3 The learning loop

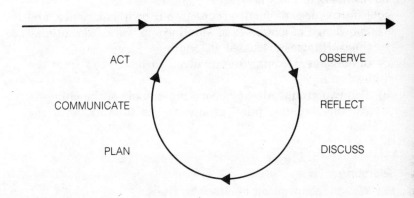

ACT OBSERVE

COMMUNICATE REFLECT

PLAN DISCUSS

Observation

(a) Relationships between youth team and kids too shallow, needed to be deeper.

(b) Clash of peer groups (usually defined by age) within the club, therefore club's difficult/tense environment.

(c) High stress levels in youth workers because of the demands of running a club.

(d) Two small groups running well outside of the club programme seen as examples of what we wanted.

Reflection

(a) Decided to pray and fast for God's new direction.

(b) We realised that we needed to be more people-oriented and less programme-oriented.

(c) No half measures seemed possible; a radical change was required.

(d) Base communities and our own experience with small groups led us to think in that direction.

Discussion

(a) The observations and reflections above were common to all members of the youth team.

(b) Effectiveness of small groups in our own experience, and knowledge of examples of small group work from around the world, was discussed at length.

(c) Management committee involved in discussion from the beginning.

(d) The two groups already operating outside of the club programme became 'pilot' groups for us to work with the observe.

Planning

(a) We made a decision to close the clubs.

(b) We fostered a relationship with the local secondary school.

(c) We decided on a name – Alpha groups – and also on how to publicise the small groups through the school.

(d) Got clearance from the school to use tutorial periods for pupils to sign up for Alpha groups.

(e) Involved young people and management committee in the planning stage.

Communication

(a) Decision made to keep management committee and young people involved all along but the implementation of the plan was left in the hands of the youth team and this was made clear to everyone involved.

(b) Team visited local churches to tell of new plan.

(c) Announcements and poster campaign in local school.

(d) Leaflet produced to explain Alpha groups to young people.

Action

(a) First week in new academic year young people sign up for Alpha groups in their tutorial periods.

(b) Allocated youth workers to groups on a first-come, first-served basis.

(c) Ran first six week programme from ideas given by young people.

(d) Daily observation and review by the team in early stages.

To put the learning loop to work for yourself, perhaps you could use the following questions for you and other workers to recognise where changes need to be made.

Observation

(a) How do you spend your time, energy, and money as a team or project?

How much time and effort goes into preparation of the programme?

. How much time and effort goes into running the programme and how much is used to follow up young people involved in the programme?

How is money spent? Do you invest in equipment programme materials, buildings (heating, lighting)? Do you pay workers? If the young people pay, what do they pay for? Analysing our use of time, energy and money will tell us where our priorities lie. Do these priorities need changing? (eg, do we need to put more time and effort into individual relationships and less into programmed events?)

(b) What do I believe God has called me to do as a youth worker?

Does this fit in with what others feel called to do in the team?

Does my calling define how I spend my time, energy and money, or does the programme, needing to be maintained, define these things?

(c) Is my effectiveness affected by stress, worries, and problems that I am currently carrying?

(d) Where are the areas of success in what I am doing that I would like to multiply?

Where are the areas of failure that I want to minimise or
remove?

Reflection

Having asked all the questions under 'Observation', what does
all this mean?
(a) Are changes needed in your use of time, energy, and money
    so that the right amounts are given to the right areas?
(b) Do some of your priorities need more time, energy, and
    money for them to function as a central part of all you do?
(c) Do any priorities need changing?
(d) Do you need to lower your expectations in some areas?
(e) Do you need to raise your expectations in some areas?
(f) Do you need to move on to something/somewhere else?
(g) Do you need to look for someone else with specific gifts to
    join your team?
(h) Are there changes in the way you do things that need to
    be implemented?

Discussion

As a team it is good to allow as much imput as possible so
that you can arrive clearly at the next change, which is to
make a plan. The questions asked in the 'Reflection' stage are
a good starting point for a discussion between yourself and
other members of your team. As well as the team, you could
ask for the involvement of:
(a) The spouses and immediate family of you and other team
    members.
(b) The leaders/elders of your church.
(c) The young people themselves.
(d) The parents of the young people.
(e) Other agencies that have regular contact with the young
    people you serve (eg, school, youth club).
  In the discussion a frank assessment of how well you are
doing is probably needed with time for both failure and success

to be fully recognised. As well as this, discussion of each person's role and calling within the team should be addressed. Stresses can be easily removed from your work if everyone is able to function within their gifting and calling.

(For a more complete assessment and review procedure, see the appendix at the end of chapter eight.)

Planning

Having answered the difficult questions of your work, you can proceed to making a plan to implement the changes that are necessary. The process for developing a strategy and vision found in the 'Frozen P's' at the end of chapter three can easily be applied at this stage.

When making a plan, certain things need to be addressed. Included in these are:

(a) The plan should allow for the calling of each worker to be exercised within the programme.

(b) The plan should be based on what we expect God to do in the future and not simply on what we have done in the past.

(c) The plan should include what we expect to see happening in one year's time with, perhaps, space for even longer-range expectations.

(d) The plan should include the means that we expect to use to get us from where we are now to where we want to be in the future. This includes new programmes, new people, new methods.

(e) The expectations that we place on each person within the team need to be included somewhere in the plan, as well as what we expect of others who support us in our work (elders, leaders, etc).

(f) Although it may be difficult at first to get a timetable right, some kind of timescale which says when things are going to happen needs to be built in.

Communication

Having made a plan, we need to ensure that everyone who needs to know, knows what is going to happen. Therefore, we ask:

(a) Who needs to know what? Is everyone who will be affected by the plan aware of what it all means?

(b) Are our expectations of others expressed to them clearly?

(c) Are there new people/new groups that we need to talk to who have not been involved in our work up to now?

Action

Finally, you need to draw up a working timetable, an action plan that tells you each day what you need to do. This timetable needs to cover the first few months so that you can hold a steady course through the early stages of implementing the new things that God has shown you. Almost immediately you will find that observation, review, and discussion are needed to help you make detailed adjustments along the way. Having been through the loop once, you will find that you will need to go through it numerous times (usually on a smaller scale) to continue the process of change. This change can truly be called repentance and faith if at every stage God is invited to take the leading part, as we ask him for his eyes, his mind, and his strength.

The process of repentance and faith

The process that I, and others with me, went through at Cambridge and Brixton was repentance and faith. We allowed observation and reflection on our experience to impact us sufficiently to make room for change. We allowed God to lead us in a fresh direction as we turned around, came to him and asked him for faith to move on.

Fig 4.4   The repentance loop for implementing A-Teams

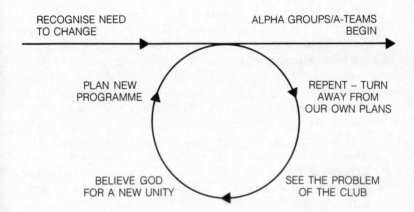

OUR YOUTH CLUB
PROGRAMME

GOD CALLING
US IN A
NEW DIRECTION

RECOGNISE NEED
TO CHANGE

ALPHA GROUPS/A-TEAMS
BEGIN

PLAN NEW
PROGRAMME

REPENT – TURN
AWAY FROM
OUR OWN PLANS

BELIEVE GOD
FOR A NEW UNITY

SEE THE PROBLEM
OF THE CLUB

We knew that God was leading us, but we had to wait for God to explain this new direction in biblical terms. This was also true of the first disciples. As they responded to the message of the kingdom, which revealed their inadequacy, they came to Jesus and followed him. But as they changed direction and trusted Jesus to lead them, they understood very little at first. It was only as they followed, asking questions along the way, that they were able to understand. This was also true of us. We could see the benefits of change but as yet we did not have a full biblical model that explained what we were doing. We had to wait for that. But it is often the case that in our discipleship of the Lord we learn 'how to' before we learn 'why'.

David Watson in his book *Discipleship* has pointed out that
Jesus trained his disciples by actively and progressively introducing them to new things: 'I do it, you do it with me, I do it
with you, you do it'. It was only towards the later stages that
the disciples began to understand what they were doing and
why. That's how Jesus still trains his disciples. Perhaps we
miss many opportunities to learn new things because we want
it all tied up before we move.

The benefits of turning round

We thought that small groups were the right direction for us
to go in, but we had no idea how much we would benefit from
using them. Small groups share various important features:

(a) **Low tech** – little or no equipment is needed to start a
    group other than what the group brings with them.
(b) **Low cost** – particularly in Brixton, the lack of equipment
    and building meant that the only costs were those the
    group chose to have. Of course full time workers are
    expensive to employ, but overall, even with full time
    workers, our costs were less than half of those of local
    authority youth clubs.
(c) **Low maintenance** – only the relationships within the
    group need to be maintained. This means that the
    maximum times and effort can be put into the groups
    without the distraction of other things.
(d) **Low stress** – with no building to police, no equipment to
    protect and no programme to produce, the youth worker is
    free of many of the stresses usually associated with youth
    work.
(e) **Good relationships** – it almost goes without saying that
    in such an ideal environment, relationships are easily fos-
    tered and grown.
(f) **Good training** – we quickly discovered that training 'on the
    job' was possible with this approach. Inexperienced workers
    could be trained by workers with more experience. In time

these inexperienced workers were often able to take on their own trainee. Coupled with informal training sessions, this approach gave us a highly effective, well trained group of workers. Even those who considered themselves to have little talent or confidence with young people found the approach sufficiently unthreatening to be included.

(g) **Responsibility and maturity** – the young people in the groups quickly took responsibility for their own programme, even to the extent of phoning workers to remind them about what was coming up that week! With responsibility came maturity as groups found it necessary to resolve relationship problems and difficulties so that the programme could function effectively.

(h) **Successful girls' work** – free from the restrictions created by having to fit in with the boys, the girls' groups created their own programmes which reflected their own ideas and needs. Today around fifty percent of all the groups are girls' groups.

(i) **Multi-racial** – since the A-Teams began in Brixton every group has been multi-racial and multi-ethnic. This interesting fact is made all the more amazing when it is realised that there have been more than forty groups formed and that the groups select their own membership. The groups seem to free young people from drawing lines of distinction between themselves and their contemporaries.

(j) **Faith sharing** – many young people (something over 100) have committed themselves to following Jesus and many have now formed a youth congregation which meets weekly at All Saints Brixton Hill.

A biblical model for A-Teams

In Matthew 10, Mark 6 and Luke 9, Jesus gives his twelve disciples a commission to go to the towns of Israel to demonstrate and proclaim the kingdom. In Luke 10 Jesus commissions the seventy-two to go and do the same giving them an identical strategy of outreach.

In these passages we see that Jesus called the disciples, authorised and empowered them to speak and act on his behalf and sent them out in twos. As they went they were not to spend time greeting friends and relations along the way, wasting valuable time. They were to go out dependent on God, which was to be expressed in their dependence on the people they were going to reach (Matthew 10:1–14, Mark 6:7–10, Luke 9:1–6, 10:17).

On arrival in a town the disciples, still in pairs, were to search for someone in the town who would listen to them. When they had found this person they were to stay with them, receiving from them whatever food and shelter the person had to offer. Having found this 'worthy person' or 'man of peace' (Matthew 10:11, Luke 10:6) they were told not to go from house to house but to preach the kingdom, heal the sick, raise the dead, cast out demons and cleanse the lepers. This prevented the disciples seeking lots of support and dissipating their time and energy in the process, and ensured that quality work was done with one household at a time.

When I first discovered this strategy I realised why it was that A-Teams seemed to be so successful – they followed the strategy for outreach which Jesus himself had given.

I realised why individual workers were rarely successful with a group and why pairs always seemed to work best. Jesus sent out his disciples in pairs.

I realised why groups were usually formed by making contact with one friendly person first who then introduced us to their peer group. The disciples were told to find a 'man of peace' who would receive them and introduce them to his household and friends.

I also realised why depending on the A-Team for the programme enabled the workers to be more successful in making friends and sharing the gospel. The disciples were told to depend on their contacts for all they needed so that their focus could be on relationships and sharing the gospel.

The process of repentance and belief had culminated in a completely new direction in our youth work and the benefits had been enormous. In time the explanation of why Jesus had led us in this direction had become clear. Our work needed to reflect more closely his strategy for outreach which he had given to his first disciples and which was still applicable today.

Since discovering this strategy we have done a lot more work on this model of outreach in the teaching of Jesus and the early church. This will be covered in the next chapter.

As disciples of Jesus struggling to come to terms with a call to reach young people with the message of the kingdom we need to adopt his starting point – repentence and belief. He will teach us as we go, as we continue in this process of turning away from our own ideas and trusting him for his.

The teaching of Jesus is applicable to every situation everywhere. Whatever style we are called to adopt, whatever the environment we find ourselves in, these basic principles apply. The process of repentance and belief will enable us to apply the changes necessary to make our work truly biblical. It will help us to implement what we hear from him and will open us up to discovering more of his ways.

How to contact young people

Few people would argue with the view that the church needs to reach more young people. We have seen that the English Church Census reveals a desperate situation. The church does not seem able either to reach or keep large numbers of young people. Even where churches have made children's work a priority, the children often leave by the time they are teenagers.

To work with young people, both children and teenagers, we need to find ways of contacting them afresh. We cannot rely on young people coming to us. Gone are the days when we could expect at least some children and teenagers to make their way into the church through family contacts or under their own steam. Young people are largely absent from the life of the local church so how do we reach out and contact them? And when we have found them, what do we do then?

People of peace on the streets

Jonathan
Jonathan and his friends used to hang around the flats on the Tilson Garden estate. There was very little to do in the area and they would often find themselves in trouble with the residents and occasionally the police. Jonathan was one of the natural leaders of the group, but the real power was in the hands of Mark and Leroy. One day as they were hanging around the car park near the flats, a couple of our youth workers walked by and started up a conversation. The workers were interested to find out who they were and what was going on in the area. As the conversation continued they realised

that they were talking to an A-Team in the making.

Introducing the idea of A-Teams wasn't particularly difficult, because the group already did everything together
anyway. All that being an A-Team meant was that they would
have the opportunity to do things that were more fun!

Steve, our senior boys worker, was given the task of forming
the group and helping it get off the ground. The first week
they met there were seventeen teenage boys present, all
between the ages of twelve and fourteen. This number didn't
include Jonathan, for at first he didn't come, but after a couple
of weeks Leroy brought him along. We didn't expect that the
group would remain at this number for very long. All our
previous experience had taught us that groups are rarely able
to function successfully at this size. But we decided to allow
the group to discover and decide this for themselves. There
were never any problems of fighting or real aggression at the
group times but the stresses and strains of it being such a
large group soon became clear.

These came to a head one day in the flats' car park. Mark
and Leroy, the two natural leaders of the group, had a fight.
No one was really clear what it was all about, but it got quite
ugly, parents were called in and the dispute spread. The first
thing that the youth workers heard about it was at the next
A-Team meeting when both Mark and Leroy were absent.
Neither of them would ever come again: one of them had lost
too much credibility and decided to go off with another set of
friends, and the other's parents prevented him from ever going
around with the group again.

With the two natural leaders gone there was a vacuum to
be filled. Jonathan, having most influence within the group,
quickly took on the role. Everyone in the group liked him and
Steve and his co-workers found him very easy to get on with.

Jonathan was a different kettle of fish to the previous
leaders. He seemed very interested to build a friendship with
Steve and almost immediately began asking 'spiritual' questions. Steve was encouraged by this and asked me what I
thought he should do. We looked at the 'man of peace' strategy

together and decided that we should assume that Jonathan wanted to know Jesus. Making this assumption was the break-through. Steve decided he would immediately begin con-sciously 'discipling' the group as they asked questions.

The very next meeting of the A-Team after our discussion became a turning point. At the end of an indoor games session, Jonathan began asking deep questions, including 'have you ever had sex?' Steve answered as fully and as frankly as he could, explaining why now as a Christian he thought that sex was something that God had given for marriage.

The conversation continued with some of the group clearly getting bored and trying to get a conversation around to foot-ball and the last international they had seen. But Jonathan was hooked. He wanted to know more about other things that God had said and how they could fit into his life. When it came time to go home Steve suggested that they should pray. To his surprise everyone agreed and he led them in a prayer about life, sex and relationships.

A few months later Jonathan made a public commitment to Christ and he and five other members of the group began an informal one to one 'basics' course. The A-Team continued to go from strength to strength. Jonathan is one of the men of peace in our community.

Ryan

Occasionally we will meet a 'person of peace' who, though clearly prepared by God, does not fit into our expectations. One such person was Ryan. We were never able to form an A-Team around him, but because we knew that he was a man of peace, we followed through anyway, and the results were quite remarkable.

I first met Ryan as he shouted over my garden fence one day and asked me whether I was the new vicar. His house was situated next door and overlooked our back garden. He said he thought it was good that someone was taking care of the garden at last! I was busy with the lawn so I didn't get involved in a conversation on that particular occasion. But a few weeks later my wife Sally said that she had had a conversation with him and thought he might be a man of peace, so I decided to follow him up.

He wasn't particularly active at the time as he had recently broken his leg in a traffic accident. Although he had friends in the area, he seemed to spend quite a lot of time by himself. His parents seemed to encourage this as they didn't always approve of the company that he kept.

We spent many hours with him individually, including him in the things we were doing that he enjoyed. He was into music and although he wasn't very good we encouraged him to 'jam' with the other musicians from the church on his newly purchased guitar. It wasn't long before Ryan became a Christian and was part of the worship team at the church. His guitar was plugged into the PA but at first we turned him down so that nobody could hear him! As he got more competent, so we turned up the volume.

Today Ryan regularly leads worship and is hoping to study classical guitar at the Royal College of Music.

We began to encourage Ryan to witness to his friends at school. He told us that there was a Christian Union and one Christian teacher on staff and so we contacted this teacher and began meeting with the Christian Union. Soon we had begun to help to run the Christian Union and put on a number of roadshows in the lunchtime. This both encouraged the Christians and drew in those who were interested in spiritual things. A number of young people became Christians from that school and although not all of them attend All Saints, most of them are involved in one local church or another.

Ryan's family became interested in his new found faith and soon his younger sister and brother were both converted. In time his mum, before conversion a self confessed atheist, and her husband both became Christians and joined the church. Through building a relationship with one person, many people were able to hear the good news.

Summary – People of peace on the streets

1 If God has called us to a group of young people there *will* be a person of peace.

2 A person of peace is recognised by the following:

   (i)   they will receive and befriend you,

   (ii) they will be a gate keeper to their group,

   (iii) they will receive your message,

   (iv) they will become Christians.

3 A person of peace will often (though not always) exhibit leadership qualities which are recognisable both before and after becoming a Christian.

4 Youth workers will need confidence and courage to make the first contact with young people on the streets.

The streets, particularly inner city streets, are an unexpectedly easy place to find young people. I have often spent time hanging around the streets with young people especially on the long warm summer evenings. Even when entering some gang's 'turf', streets are sufficiently neutral to make it possible to have a conversation. I always make it clear who I am and that I just want to talk but still it requires courage, determination and consistency. But there on the streets it is possible to make contacts 'from cold' that we might otherwise never make. The biggest barrier to doing this is usually in ourselves – we all feel scared!

Confidence to make contact

Calling

The real basis of confidence in Christian youth work, like any other work in the kingdom, lies in God's calling. It is important to know we are called to be Christian youth workers. Calling is clarified in a number of ways. First we need to have some sense of God speaking to us personally. This should be part and parcel of our everyday life. God is a God who speaks. We will hear God speaking through Scripture, prayer, the body of

Christ and the world around. It should of course always be tested against Scripture and weighed by others as we share with our church leaders and other brothers and sisters in the church. If we hear God's voice we will hear his call.

If God calls us we can be sure that his strength is available to fulfil the call even though we may be weak. Scripture is full of examples of people who, having received the call of God, were enabled to fulfil his mission for their lives. Abraham, Moses, Joshua, Gideon and David all heard God's call and were enabled to fulfil it as they obeyed.

Commissioning

As well as calling there is also commissioning. This comes as God brings together circumstances that confirm not only *the calling in general* but also *the timing in particular*.

For instance, Gideon knew he was called to lead Israel against the Midianites, but the timing was dictated by God creating low morale among the Midianite forces and revealing it to Gideon (Judges 7:8–15). Gideon was able to say to the Israelite soldiers as he returned from spying on the Midianite camp, 'Get up! the Lord has given the Midianite camp into your hands'. Likewise Nehemiah knew that God had called him to rebuild the walls of Jerusalem, but the timing was confirmed as the king gave him the resources to do it. He was able to go to Jerusalem and say:

> 'You see the trouble we are in: Jerusalem lies in ruins, and its gates have been burned with fire. Come, let us rebuild the wall of Jerusalem, and we will no longer be in disgrace.' I also told them about the gracious hand of my God upon me and what the king had said to me. They replied, 'Let us start rebuilding.' So they began this good work (Nehemiah 2:v17–18).

Nehemiah recognised that the circumstances were the evidence of God's gracious hand upon him. In other words, he could have confidence because he knew God was going ahead of him to prepare the way.

We also need to know that we are called. We should ask God to speak to us clearly as we pray, read Scripture and submit what we are hearing to the body of Christ. As the sense of call grows, so will our confidence.

Along with this, our awareness of commissioning will come as we see God confirming his call through the circumstances of our lives. Even Jesus, sent by God with the highest calling of all, waited for the right time to begin his work, marked by his baptism at the beginning of his ministry. We need to be able to recognise God's provision and commissioning for ministry.

Whether this is short term ministry to one group of kids, or a long term ministry extending over the whole of our lives, we need to know the signs. For instance, when we contact a new group of young people, we should allow God to direct us through circumstances as to whether we should commit time and energy to the group. One of the ways that we will know is by recognising a person of peace. If we are received, befriended and welcomed, our initial assumption can be that God has gone ahead of us, preparing the way, both for us and for the message of the kingdom.

Summary – Calling and commissioning
1 Our confidence is in God's calling, not our ability as a youth worker
2 We will recognise God's call as we listen to him through Scripture, prayer and the church
3 The timing of our call will depend on God's commissioning
4 We will know God's commissioning as he provides the opportunities and resouces to fulfil the call

People of peace in the schools

Carmen
Carmen is a 'woman of peace'. She was contacted by the youth team taking assemblies and running lunchtime roadshows at the local Church of England senior girls' school. She, along

with a number of others, formed an A-Team, which although functional, was never a roaring success. When the group eventually split, Carmen formed a new group with her good friend Elizabeth. Beccy, our senior girls worker, led the group with a variety of co-workers. In time Carmen became a Christian, so did Elizabeth and a number of others in the group.

Carmen, now seventeen, is preparing to lead her own A-Team of younger girls from the same school. She is not only one of the women of peace at her school, but a key member of the seven o'clock congregation at All Saints.

Even though Carmen's A-Team did not work particularly well at first, Beccy and the other workers were able to persist. They could see real receptivity in Carmen and therefore good reason to spend their time and energy in working through the problems.

To contact young people we will need to go to the places that they go to. The schools are an obvious place to start; despite the truancy rate, most young people still go to school. It was a Scripture Union worker who first challenged us to get involved in schools. 'If you really want to contact young people go to where you can find them in great numbers every day of the week,' he said. It will require time free during the day and special skills to work in assemblies and at lunch time meetings. But if we are concerned to reach young people then we should include the schools as a vital part of our overall strategy. Nowhere else are we presented with so many opportunities to meet so many young people.

Tony

Like Carmen, Tony was contacted through our schools programme, as members of our youth team went into one of the local senior schools for morning assemblies and lunchtime roadshows.

It had taken some time to cultivate a good working relationship with the school, who were a little suspicious of what a group of Christian youth workers might be wanting to do. After the first few assemblies, the principal loosened the reins a little and allowed us in at lunchtime. Here we would set up a sound system and play contemporary music, organise trust and communication games with such things as parachutes and earth balls, and talk with the pupils.

As always we were looking for people who liked us, who wanted to spend time with us and who seemed to have a basic receptivity towards us. Tony was one such person. He would turn up every time we came in and we began to build a good relationship with him. The principal and staff, realising we were not there to preach long sermons or hand out Bible tracts, began to trust us a little more. When we suggested that we might form a mixed American Football team in the school they warmed to the idea. Tony signed up and was quickly recognised as a key player.

Once the training period was over he was asked to be team captain, which he took on with enthusiasm. He was well liked by both staff and pupils, was an excellent morale builder and a good enough sportsman to provide the right sort of leadership.

The team were runners up in the mini league that year, and Tony was presented with the prize for being the team's 'most valuable player'. He was presented with his trophy at the end of season banquet at which a number of Christian professional football players from the North American Football League spoke. Through them God began to challenge the players to think about more than themselves and their sporting achievements. Tony would soon discover that there was something more important than being the team's most valuable player.

At the Easter training camp, Tony and his team joined the other teams as we went off for a weekend in the country. The weekend was led by Steve Connors, the Christian coach of the Oxford Bulldogs, and by Mark Tedder, our own senior schools worker. Both are American and their accent seemed to give them the credibility they needed!

Over the weekend Tony decided to commit himself to following Jesus and he and his 'huddle' all decided to learn more of what it was to be a Christian. Tony is one of our men of peace in the schools with which we have contact. The workers who contacted Tony knew they were called, and recognised God's commissioning for ministry as they saw in Tony a young man prepared by God.

Summary – People of peace in the schools

1 If God has called us to a group of young people there will be a person of peace

2 A person of peace is recognised by the following:
   (i)   they will receive and befriend you
   (ii) they will be a gate keeper to their group
   (iii) they will receive your message
   (iv) they will become Christians

3 A person of peace will often (though not always) exhibit leadership qualities which are recognisable both before and after becoming a Christian

4 Youth workers will need to develop particular skills in public communication if they are to do school assemblies

5 To do roadshow style events in playgrounds or gyms, youth workers will need crowd gathering ideas, eg games, music, drama

6 Youth workers will need to watch the crowd at assemblies, etc, for possible people of peace and have the confidence to speak to them afterwards

More about people of peace

As we saw in the previous chapter, our strategy for A-Teams is based upon the mission strategy of Jesus as recorded in the gospels. This strategy operates as the focus for all our evangelistic strategy in Brixton and across south London. It provides us with a method by which we can contact, network, serve and evangelise young people and every other age group in our community.

The key component of this strategy is the identification of what Jesus called the 'man of peace'. This person, either male or female, who may also be called a 'worthy person' (Matthew

10:11) is the way into the relationships God has prepared for us.

When Jesus was teaching his disciples this strategy of evangelism, and what to expect in response from others, he seemed to assume that those who receive us receive him also: 'He who receives you receives me, and he who receives me receives the one who sent me' (Matthew 10:40).

If this is as true today as it was then, it means that we can expect to find a man of peace, or worthy person in each group we are sent to those who will become followers of Jesus. This expectation has been so regularly fulfilled in my experience that I feel sure it is the right way to approach evangelism in any context. Jonathan and Carmen became Christians because God called them. As youth workers we were able to recognise this by the way they received us as people and our message of good news.

Paul, someone who had never met Jesus during his ministry, or heard the strategy first hand, used precisely the same methods as he planted churches in the major cities around the Mediterranean. First he teamed up with a partner, Barnabas, and then Silas. Obviously there were other members of the team, but he always seemed to have a co-worker. He went out totally reliant on God, supported by his skills as a tent maker. He later made the point, when writing to one of his churches, that this was an unusual practice for apostles and other travelling ministers who would normally, like the twelve and the seventy-two, seek support from those they visited. His dependence upon God was expressed in a different way as he obeyed the Lord in the particular lifestyle that he developed as a church planter (1 Corinthians 9:1–15).

On arrival in a city he searched first for the responsive people, beginning in the synagogues and then beyond. In Philippi Paul arrived for the first time in a Roman Colony City, mainly Latin speaking, which was without a synagogue. As a synagogue could have been formed with ten adult male Jews, we are led to the conclusion that Paul's usual starting point – the Jewish community – was not available. Paul was in new and unfamiliar territory. It is probably for this reason that Luke decided to explain more fully how Paul was able to establish a church using his normal methods of evanglism in unfamiliar surroundings. He searched for a man of peace and found a woman, Lydia, praying with some others by a river outside the city gate. She was a Greek-speaking God-fearer. She heard and received his message and invited him to form a church in her home. Although Paul adapted some parts of the strategy to his own calling and environment, it is basically the same one which Jesus gave to the twelve and the seventy-two.

Having planted the Philippian church out of relationships, following the strategies of Jesus, Paul was confident that the church would continue to grow and mature in the gospel they had received:

> In all my prayers for all of you, I always pray with joy because of your partnership in the gospel from the first day until now, being confident of this, that he who began a good work in you will carry it on to completion until the day of Christ Jesus (Philippians 1:4–6).

Paul was confident even though he had not been able to spend very long with this infant church. This was because God had started something, and Paul knew he would finish it. Because Paul had learned to recognise the signs of God preparing the way for the gospel, which included the presence of a person of peace, he could be confident about the outcome.

In whatever situation we find ourselves in, and whatever environment or style of youth work we are called to work within, we should always look for these key receptive people – the men and women of peace. They truly are the 'gate-keepers' of what God intends to do in groups and communities. Unless we recognise their vital role, we may miss the work which God has prepared in advance for us to do.

Being a youth worker in the kingdom of God is difficult enough; but if we don't use the opportunities God provides, it becomes impossible.

Making progress

This section presents a method of charting our progress as we make contact with our 'person of peace' and draw them into a relationship that will eventually lead them to the Lord.

Here we visualise ourselves as being at the centre of a series of concentric circles. At the centre of these circles with us is God, our relationship with him being the centre and focus of all we do. Moving out from this centre, there are different kinds of relationships, beginning with the relationships with people with whom we are closest and ending with those with whom we have least contact.

Alternatively, we can visualise ourselves and our 'person of peace' at the centre of a series of concentric circles. The difference is that we have a relationship with God through Jesus Christ, and they do not (or certainly do not recognise that they have one, if they do). Our objective is to invite our 'person of peace' into our most personal and intimate relationship; the one that we have with the Lord. As they do this, they will have God at the centre of their lives as well, and share the same centre and focus that we have.

We first contact our 'person of peace' at the level of the outermost ring of personal relationships, and then we invite them into the next ring, which is the circle of friends that we share. Of course they, too, will invite us into their circle of friends, and this would be the opportunity to establish an A-Team with them and their peer group. At this point, we are sharing in their friendships, and they are sharing in ours. The next stage is to invite your 'person of peace' to share in family relationships so that they feel comfortable and welcomed in your home. At the same time, you will need to make the same contacts with their family and home.

By now the 'person of peace' is ready to meet the one with whom you share your most intimate relationships – the Lord himself.

Following this approach means that we always work through relationship and never try to invent a programme through which we try to convert people. And, in addition, we pass on to the new convert at the earliest stage the best method of evangelism. My wife, Sally, has used this approach to good effect in the lives of a number of women. She decides where her 'woman of peace' is in terms of her circle of relationships and then encourages them to move to the next.

Although the whole approach seems to take quite a while, the people that she has evangelised through this method have all remained very secure in their faith and in the knowledge they have of Christ.

Think of any 'people of peace' that you know and place them, mentally, at the appropriate place within your own concentric circles of relationships. When you have done this, pray that God will give you the opportunity to invite them into the next circle and that they will respond postively to the invitation as you allow the Lord to develop the relationship which he has called into being.

GET GOING!

Crowd gathering games

I have included a number of the most successful crowd gathering games that we have used in schools over the years. To gather a crowd you need to raise awareness of your presence in the people present and raise the level of curiosity in the people to the extent that they want to become involved.

To do this we have used earthballs. These are nine foot in diameter inflatable balls which you can use to play all sorts of games, like King of the World, where one person tries to stay balanced on top of the ball for the longest, while the others watch.

We have also found parachute games are particularly good at gathering a crowd. Parachute games usually go under the general description of trust and communication games – they help the people playing the games to have fun and open up to one another.

Here are just a few examples:

Mushroom. First gather a group of people around the parachute with everyone holding a parachute at waist height. Ask
everyone to crouch holding the parachute. Get everyone to
stand up fast, pulling the parachute over their heads and
taking one step in (to allow the chute to balloon more).

Variations: (1) once parachute mushrooms, all run into
           middle.
          (2) once parachute mushrooms, all clap, turn
           around, etc.

Mushroom swap. When the chute mushrooms, call out who
is to swap places (all wearing blue, etc).

Blast off. This is the same as 'Mushroom' except with a ball
on top of the chute. See how high it goes.

Jaws. Sit around holding the chute, waving it slightly to give
a wave effect. Someone goes underneath and is the shark. The
shark grabs the ankle of one of the seated players who goes
down under the chute with a shriek. They are now both sharks
and the game continues until everyone is a shark!

Trust and communication games

Having gathered a crowd using a parachute, earthball or perhaps music through a PA, you can move to other more intimate
trust and communication games. The objective of these games
for the youth worker is to build up relationships with the
young people. Be sure to look for the most receptive ones and
those who may be the men and women of peace.

Here are a selection of some of the best games, with an
indicator of the age groups, they are suitable for:

People lift (12–20). A volunteer lies on the ground on her
back and folds her arms across her chest. The rest make a
circle around her, place their hands underneath her body and

raise her to waist height, then to shoulders and then above heads. This can also be done with two groups, swapping the volunteers between groups. It is easier and much less embarrassing for the volunteers if this is done by swapping the supporters while the two people remain standing, unless of course you want to go in for a bit of human juggling.

Sit down (12+). Everyone stands in a circle, shoulder to shoulder. Then all turn to their right. Make sure the circle is tight by getting people to take steps in towards the centre. When there are no gaps, on the count of three everyone sits down on the lap of the person behind them. Once they have managed this, you can try getting everyone to raise their outside leg and see how long they can hold it.

Spiral (12+). Everyone stands in a circle. It is broken at one point and one end goes to the centre of circle. The person at the other end starts walking so as to wrap the spiral tightly round the person in the middle. It is important that the person in the middle doesn't turn round. When the spiral is wrapped tight the person in the centre ducks down and starts to make their way out through the forest of legs. The rest of the group follows down and through until they are completely uncoiled.

Knots (12+). Circles of at least eight people. Tell them each to take hold of two other hands, not belonging to the same person or to the people next to them. The idea is then to untangle the knot.

Knots II (12+). Circles of six to eight people holding hands. Get them to number themselves around the circle. The leader calls out instructions to be obeyed until the groups are completely tangled, eg, 'number six place their right foot over number two's left arm'.

Wind in the Willows (6–12). Make tight circle (no more than eight or ten). One person in middle closes eyes, folds arms across chest and relaxes. Standing dead in the centre with feet together, they are pushed around the circle.

Wibbly wobbly (20+). Four or five teams of about eight people line up at one end with one person for each team at the other end holding a hockey stick. On 'Go' the first person runs to the other end, places their forehead on the hockey stick and turns round ten times then runs back to their team. It then carries on as a relay. For interesting alternatives try hopping or closing eyes (or both!) on the return journey. Watch out for safety.

People pass (20+). In pairs of similar height. Arrange all the pairs in a long line, roughly in height order with the smallest at the front. The volunteer, preferably small, is hoisted up onto the top of the line at the front and is passed along the line of people who act as a conveyor belt with their arms in the air. If well supervised it is safe and good fun.

Fallback (Any age). In pairs. One falls back and is caught firmly beneath the arms by the other.

Star wars (12–20). Divide the playing area into two with a line. Place several death stars (more commonly known as sponge balls) along this line. Two armies take up positions in their area and choose one of their number to be a Jedi Knight armed with a Light Sabre that looks uncannily like a rolled up newspaper. The armies rush to the dividing line and collect death stars which they hurl at the opposition. The Jedi Knight remains on base (marked out by a hoop in each area). If a member of any army is hit by a death star then they are frozen to the spot. They can only be released by their Jedi Knight who must come and touch them with the Light Saber. He may also use this to fend off death stars. If the Jedi Knight is hit then that army has lost altogether. The game obviously revolves around the protection of the Jedi Knight.

A three dimensional lifestyle

One of the biggest pressures of being a youth worker is that our ideas are so quickly used up. Youth workers are always in the market for new ideas – before long we need fresh input from somewhere to us keep going.

The pressure always to come up with new ideas is partly removed by ensuring that we are not in a provider-client relationship, where we are always to 'lay something on' for the young people. Removing the provider-client relationship lifts much of the pressure of programming. But still our work needs creativity and direction and we need to be able to think through the best way to implement good practice. A-teams is one way of working with teenagers, but there may be another way for you.

Coming up with these new ideas and fresh ways of interpreting and implementing fundamental principles is a vital skill for us all. Creativity is not a mystery, nor is it something only available to some. To be creative requires two things. Both of them need to be part of our lifestyle and both arise from our discipleship to Jesus. The first is the process of repentance and faith which we explored earlier in the book. The second is the subject of this chapter – a three dimensional lifestyle.

Repentance and faith

First things first. As we have seen, repentance is important because it turns a person around and brings about an openness which is vital if new ideas are to be created. It also does something else which is very important: it brings them to Jesus, the author of all the best ideas.

Left to our own devices we would always tend to seek our

own way. Repentance puts us back on his way. When I go with my family to visit my Mum and Dad, I can occasionally be found playing bowls with my Dad at the local 'crown green' grass bowls club. When I first started to play I found it difficult to get used to the idea that the bowls were weighted on one side. I could never get them to go in a straight line! Like the wooden bowls, or 'woods', in the game, we have an inbuilt bias – sin – which makes us veer off the track. Only God can keep us on the straight and narrow.

As we develop a relationship with him, he is able to reveal the pitfalls and problems and keep us close to him. As we cooperate, maintaining our side of the relationship, he shows us how to stay in the process of repentance and faith by teaching us a new lifestyle – a lifestyle with repentance and faith built in. We need a lifestyle which enables us to continue to develop and try the new things he wants to show us.

The first disciples learned this new lifestyle as they turned away from their old life, followed Jesus and took on his. When Peter was first exposed to the kingdom as Jesus preached from his boat and gave him a great catch of fish, his response was to fall on his knees and say, 'Go away from me, Lord; I am a sinful man!' But Jesus said, 'Don't be afraid; from now on you will catch men.' And the outcome was that Peter and the others, 'pulled their boats up on shore, left everything and followed him' (Luke 5:8–11).

Repentance paved his way for new things. As soon as Peter had repented and turned away from his old life, Jesus gave him a new idea, a new plan, a new programme – fishing for men. For us to be able to get ideas that work, we need to be sure they are God's ideas. When the disciples came to Jesus they found a man who could lead and teach them, not only by what he said, but by how he lived. 'They followed him', means they committed themselves to him unconditionally and took on his way of doing things. This is the key to all good new ideas.

In time, repentance and faith were built into the lifestyle of the disciples. After each programme – each outward expression of life – they returned to Jesus and assessed what they had done. To return to Jesus is to repent. Sometimes we repent of sin and failure, sometimes we simply 'return' after activity to find our rest in him.

An example of simply 'returning' to Jesus to reassess, relax and recharge is found in the story of the twelve returning from their preaching mission in Mark 6:30–31:

> The apostles gathered round Jesus and reported to him all they had done and taught. Then, because so many people were coming and going that they did not even have a chance to eat, he said to them, 'Come with me by yourselves to a quiet place and get some rest.'

They didn't get much of a chance to rest on that particular occasion because the crowd followed them. The feeding of the five thousand was the result. But Jesus clearly intended the twelve to draw aside with him and rest.

An example of repentance following failure is found in the story of the disciples attempting to cast a demon from an epileptic boy. Their failure drove them back to Jesus and this repentance – turning to the Lord – resulted in the boy being healed and them learning something new (Luke 11:37–43).

Failure, whether it is real or imagined, is often a good spur to repentance. When the youth clubs at the Romsey Mill were not working in the way we wanted them to, it drove us back to God for a solution. Failure drives us into the arms of the Father and he is able to show us in his Son what we need to do. We learn from him and his lifestyle what new things we need to include in our life and work.

Jesus and the three dimensional life
Jesus lived a three dimensional lifestyle. He lived in constant submission and worship to his Father (the first dimension). He lived for his disciples, sharing his life and walking with them (the second dimension). He proclaimed the kingdom, serving others and bearing witness daily to what he knew (the third dimension).

His life was defined by the *upward* dimension of worship, the *inward* dimension of relationship to his followers and the *outward* dimension of witness to the world.

Fig 6.1

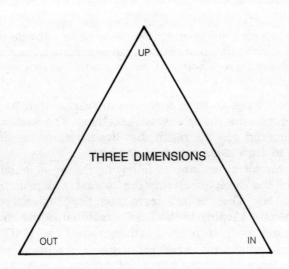

As we read the gospels, the three dimensional lifestyle of Jesus comes across clearly. Luke 6:12–20 reads like this:

UP   One of those days Jesus went out to a mountainside to pray, and spent the night praying to God.

IN   When morning came, he called his disciples to him and chose twelve of them, whom he also designated apostles . . .

OUT   A large crowd of his disciples was there and a great number of people from all over Judea, from Jerusalem, and from the coast of Tyre and Sidon, who had come to hear him and to be healed of their diseases. Those troubled by evil spirits were cured, and the people all tried to touch him, because power was coming from him and healing them all. Looking at his disciples, he said: 'Blessed are you who are poor, for yours is the kingdom of God.'

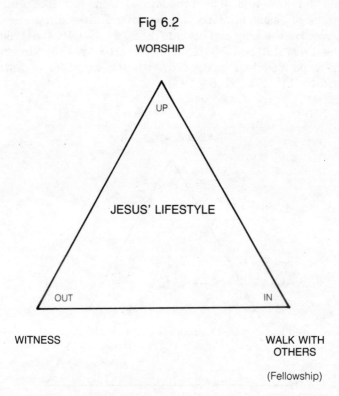

Fig 6.2

WORSHIP

UP

JESUS' LIFESTYLE

OUT

IN

WITNESS

WALK WITH OTHERS

(Fellowship)

Jesus taught his disciples this lifestyle so that his life became their model and their life a reflection of his. As he trained them, this three dimensional lifestyle affected every part of their experience, both large and small. They too became conditioned by an 'Up In Out' way of doing things. God came first in worship and prayer, fellow disciples next in a shared life and common purse, and finally their service of others as they lived out the kingdom of God.

The three dimensional teaching of Jesus

The kingdom

The three dimensional view of life affected everything that
Jesus did and said. The kingdom of God was the central
message of Jesus' ministry and was itself three dimensional,
composed of the king and his rule (Luke 23:3 – UP), the subject
of the king (Matthew 5:3 – IN) and the activity of the kingdom
as it expanded and contended with the kingdom of Satan
(Matthew 11:12–13:31–3 – OUT).

Fig 6.3

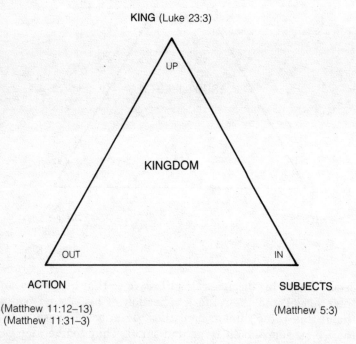

KING (Luke 23:3)

UP

KINGDOM

OUT   IN

ACTION   SUBJECTS

(Matthew 11:12–13)   (Matthew 5:3)
(Matthew 11:31–3)

Prayer

The three dimensions affected all other areas of Jesus' teaching as well. The 'Lord's Prayer' or probably more accurately,
the 'Disciples' Prayer', is a good example:

UP   Our Father in heaven, hallowed be your name, your kingdom come, you will be done on earth as it is in heaven. Give us today our daily bread. Forgive us our debts,

IN   as we also have forgiven our debtors.

OUT   but deliver us from the evil one.

Fig 6.4

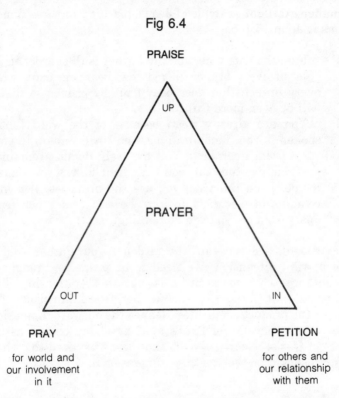

PRAISE

UP

PRAYER

OUT   IN

PRAY   PETITION

for world and   for others and
our involvement   our relationship
in it   with them

In our prayer we should first recognise God for who he is – our holy Father, King and Lord, and provider and forgiver of our sins. Second, we should recognise the need to maintain good relationships with those around us through forgiveness. Third, we should seek God's help as we go out into the world,

that he keep us pure and safe from the enemy. Even prayer
is 'Up In Out'. We should pray in three dimensions: pray UP
in praise and recognition of God, IN about relationships with
others, OUT as we pray for the world and others.

The church – 'the vine'

Another excellent example of Jesus' teaching in three dimensions is John 15:1–5:

UP   I am the true vine, and my Father is the gardener. He
      cuts off every branch in me that bears no fruit, while
      every branch that does bear fruit he prunes so that it
      will be even more fruitful.
IN   You are already clean because of the word I have
      spoken to you. Remain in me, and I will remain in you.
OUT   No branch can bear fruit by itself; it must remain in
      the vine. Neither can you bear fruit unless you remain
      in me. I am the vine; you are the branches. If a man
      remains in me and I in him, he will bear much fruit;
      apart from me you can do nothing.

The true vine – Jesus – and the gardener – our Father – define
the upward dimension. We need to be pruned – brought to
repentance – to maintain this upward relationship. The
branches – all Christians – define the inward dimension. The
fruit – the product of our life – defines the outward dimension.
The vine, a parallel of Paul's analogy of the church as the
body of Christ, clearly reveals that Jesus believed the whole
church should be seen as three dimensional.

Paul's teaching in the New Testament

Other parts of Scripture underline the three dimensions. One
example is found in Ephesians. Watchman Nee expounds this
superbly in his short commentary, *Sit, Walk, Stand*.
    The whole book of Ephesians explains and underlines the
importance of a three dimensional lifestyle.

Fig 6.5

SIT (Ephesians 2)

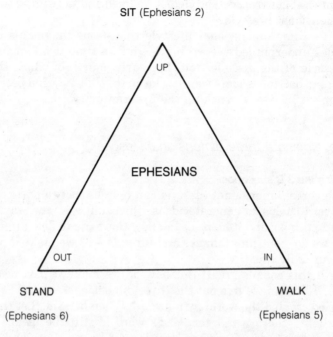

STAND   WALK

(Ephesians 6)   (Ephesians 5)

We are *seated* with Christ in the heavenly realms. By faith we receive all the benefits of his finished work, completed as he sat down on his heavenly throne having lived, died and risen for us. We *walk* in a new life now that Christ has freed us from our old life, which led to death. We *stand* against Satan our enemy, and see him defeated.

Ephesians is an exposition of UP IN OUT, so much so that even individual verses are shot through with this understanding:

UP   From him the whole body,
IN   joined and held together by every supporting ligament, grows and guilds itself up in love,
OUT as each part does its work (Ephesians 4:16).

Paul was one of the church's most important thinkers and leaders. Though not one of 'the twelve', he was part of the post Pentecost generation, and clearly he lived and taught the three dimensional lifestyle.

The three dimensional lifestyle that Jesus taught his disciples underpinned everything he did. In time it became the lifestyle of the disciples too. The early church of which they were to become leaders was to take on this lifestyle and become highly effective in reaching the first century world.

Developing a three dimensional lifestyle

Using the 3 D's as a tool

The three dimensional lifestyle can help us in two particular ways: it helps to generate ideas which initiate new ways of doing things; and it helps us to allow God's life to flow through all we do – our programmes and lifestyle – as we make it part of our daily life.

All this sounds great! But how do we make it part of our life? How can we live out the three dimensions?

God created the world by his word. When he said, 'Let there be light', there was light. God's word is still the means by which he creates. If we are to reflect God's creativity and life in our lives, we need first to listen to his creative word.

The three dimensional lifestyle begins with turning to God. We come to him wanting to hear his word about what we are doing. This is the *upward* dimension. We continue as we interpret the word through contact and conversation with our Christian brothers and sisters. This is the *inward* dimension. The word is applied as we respond and do something about what we have heard and understood. This is the *outward* dimension. As we do this, new ideas are generated and God's creative answers are found. Like Jesus and the first disciples we live by hearing God's word, understanding what it means and applying it in our everyday life (Matthew 4:4). (See Fig 6.6 on page 105.)

Fig 6.6

REVELATION

God Revealing
Himself – Word

UP

REVELATION

OUT   IN

RESPONSE

on the basis of
application of the
interpreted word

RELATIONSHIP

where we work
out interpretation
of word

Two practical examples

In the story of Alpha group and A-Teams the development of the three dimensional process can be seen operating and producing new ideas. We turned to God and repented of our previous ways of doing things and sought his direction. He gave us a *revelation* of a new way of working. This was *interpreted* – 'worked out' within the team and in the relationships that existed between us and the young people. It was *applied* by starting the new programme. (See Fig 6.7 on page 106.)

Outside In

Fig 6.7

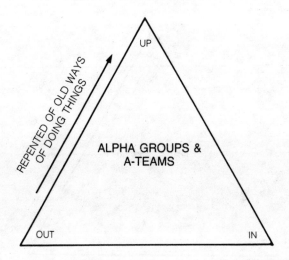

LISTENED FOR GOD'S
FRESH REVELATION
OF SMALL GROUPS

REPENTED OF OLD WAYS
OF DOING THINGS

UP

ALPHA GROUPS &
A-TEAMS

OUT

IN

STARTED NEW PROGRAMME:
ALPHA GROUPS/A-TEAMS

INTERPRETED
REVELATION OF SMALL
GROUPS IN YOUTH TEAM
& YOUNG PEOPLE

In Brixton God revealed to us the biblical model of A-Teams in the outreach strategy of Jesus. The strategy is itself three dimensional. Jesus gave *revelation* in the form of a commission and a clear target – a town in Israel. This was *interpreted* – worked out in relationships, first in the relationship between the disciples he sent out in pairs, and then in the relationship with the 'man of peace'. The *application* came as the disciples obeyed Jesus and proclaimed the kingdom, healed the sick, raised the dead, cast out demons and cleansed the lepers. (See Fig 6.8 on page 107.)

Fig 6.8

JESUS REVEALED TASK
AND MISSION TARGETS

DISCIPLES RETURNED

UP

DISCIPLES OBEYED

MISSION
STRATEGY OF
JESUS

OUT   IN

TASK APPLIED
AND ACCOMPLISHED

TASK WORKED OUT
IN 'PAIRS' AND WITH
MAN OF PEACE

Creative and successful

Understanding new ideas, new direction and fresh revelation as primarily God's work takes away much of the pressure we feel to be creative and successful. God has all the good ideas, all the best programmes. All we have to do is find out what they are! We do this by living the life that is revealed in his Son.

Everything we need, all the new ideas are prepared in advance. He knows what will work best and what will produce the results we desire, and he has them all ready for us! In Ephesians, Paul tells us that we are saved by grace – God's free gift – and we also live and work by grace – God's free gift –

'Good works' and 'God works': 'For we are God's workmanship, created by Christ Jesus to do good works, which God prepared in advance for us to do' (Ephesians 2:10).

Being creative does not mean that we cannot use other people's ideas. Often God's revelation will come to us through the things that others have discovered. In his book, *Leadership and Church Growth*, Peter Wagner has pointed out that we need to learn to *adapt* other people's ideas, rather than simply *adopt* them. We may find it difficult to generate our own ideas at first; genuinely new ideas seem to be few and far between. But if we implement the three dimensional process we will learn to adapt other people's ideas as we interpret and apply the revelation that we find in them. We will also more than likely find that our creativity grows as we continue to integrate this process into our lives.

Whether we start with our ideas or the ideas of others, our part is to listen to God, receiving the revelation he has for us, interpreting it among other believers and applying it in the situation we find ourselves in. If we are confused and at a loss, we can be sure he isn't. It may be that we do not get all we need the first time we start to live out the three dimensional life. We should continue. As we continue in the cycle returning to him and repenting of our failures, he will help us gradually to improve our work.

Problem solving and the All Saints programme

I have learned to use the three dimensions as a way of problem solving when things seem to be going wrong. If some part of the programme seems to be faltering I immediately ask myself: Are the three dimensions being expressed or are we missing one? For example, if one of the young people's fellowship groups (which will be described in the next chapter) seems to be in trouble, I always check whether they are expressing the three dimensions.

'Are they giving time and energy to worship and prayer?' (UP)
'Are they giving time and energy to developing the relationships in the group?' (IN)
'Are they giving time and energy to reaching out and serving
others?' (OUT)

The answers to these simple questions often reveal where the
problem lies.

If an A-Team seems to be hitting problems I ask similar
questions:

'Was the group revealed by God by the presence of a "person
of peace?" "Are the youth workers praying for the group?" '
(UP)
'Does the group resolve conflicts?' 'Do the workers spend time
making friends?' (IN)
'Does the group have an outgoing programme or are they
sitting around?' (OUT)

The overall goal is to ensure that as a whole the
development of our programme reflects this centrally important three dimensional principle. We hope that as we seek to
reflect the three dimensional lifestyle of Jesus, the programme
supports this teaching. The programme can be used as visual
aid of what we believe!

Conclusion

Having reflected on this process for a number of years, I am
convinced that it is the only guarantee to successful, creative
and worthwhile youth work. In fact, it forms the foundation
of all that the church is called to do. The development of a
youth congregation among the other congregations which
make up the church of All Saints was dependent on this principle. So has been the development of all the church's youth
work, from the children's programme to that for older teenagers.

If only we would build in an upward, inward and outward dimension into all we do, we would see the life and creativity of God flowing through everything we do. Making this a pattern for life would ensure that we would continue to learn from God the new things he wants to show us.

The next chapter continues the theme of the three dimensions and applies them to the subject of worship, fellowship and the communication of the gospel.

Worship, pastoral care and communication

The drum machine started. Steve – looking like he might have just come from 'The Fridge', a well known night club in Brixton, picked up a mike and began to rap . . .

I bet you're wonderin' why we're here today
and even more what I'm going to say
One thing I know is that we are all believers
Come together in the name of Jesus . . .

God has put real love in our lives
and we don't look like we're trying to survive . . .

Get yourself grounded in the word of truth
Yeah, that's right – reading, listening, praying
Learning from God and doing what he's saying
We're not here just to 'do the right thing'
know what I'm saying . . .

We are JAMMIN!
JAMMIN!
This means . . .
Jesus **a**nd **m**e **m**akin' **i**mpact **n**ow
JAMMIN!
You, and me we're gonna learn how by
JAMMIN!

Though unfamiliar to many Christians as a 'call to worship', that is precisely how this rap was used one evening as our youth congregation gathered.

Culture, environment, education and other factors, will influence the style of worship, but the basic content should be the same. Christian worship will contain the same basic elements that unite it with all other Christian worship around the world.

As I write (in 1992) All Saints has at least five different
styles of worship on any given Sunday. The informal though
traditionally structured Morning Prayer, and the very informal Family Service take place on a Sunday morning. The
Youth Congregation and the service conducted by the 'Faith
and Victory' Church take place in the afternoon. At 7.00 p.m.
the Evening Congregation meets. Added to these there is the
children's service, 'The Radical Angel Club' (RAC!), which
meets on a Thursday evening and the United Teaching Service
which meets later on the same evening. Taking all of these
into account there are probably five or six styles of worship,
which all represent All Saints Church. Although the styles
may be different, the main elements of all this worship remain
the same. If we broaden the picture to look at London or any
other large cosmopolitan city, Christians are worshipping in
perhaps hundreds of different ways.

A youth congregation

Young people represent a specific group within our society –
a 'sub-culture' – and as such their worship will look, sound
and 'feel' different to the worship which adults prefer. Also,
young people tend to have specific characteristics and particular group identities that mark them off from other young
people within the wider group or sub-culture to which they
belong. All of these factors will contribute to worship among
young people being different. Other age groups and sub-
cultures will worship in a different way to them. It is always
a mistake to 'lift' worship happening in one place and among
one group and impose it on another.

Even lifting youth worship from one place to another can
be a misguided. When we were planning to start our own youth
congregation we took a group of young people and leaders to
St Thomas' Crookes in Sheffield. St Thomas' was known for
having broken new ground in the whole area of worship and
young people. So we travelled up one Sunday taking a number
of young people and leaders with us. Many of the leaders

enjoyed what they saw and had a great experience, but driving home down the M1 in the church minibus the young people were noticeably quiet. At first I put this down to tiredness but when I asked a few what they thought of the worship, the reaction was very strong and very negative! It was definitely not what they were looking for! Their main worry was that we were going to set up our Sunday service in that way.

The experience served to show me that however 'right' and good one particular way of doing things may be for others, however effective it is in one context, as St Thomas' 9.00 service undoubtedly is, it may not be transferable to somewhere else either in whole or in part.

Basic parameters of worship

When seeking to develop worship within a youth context it is important to establish two boundaries. The first parameter is that:

> worship should contain all the major elements of Christian worship revealed in Scripture and practised in all the major streams and traditions of the Christian church.

This means that praise and thanksgiving, confession of sin, reflection on Scripture, prayer, giving, the Lord's supper and a commissioning for service in the world should regularly form part of our corporate worship. Perhaps not every element needs to be present every time, but they should all be included regularly and often.

The second parameter is that:

> worship should be accessible and 'at the level' of the group who are worshipping.

This means that worship should be in a language, form and style that is understood and accessible to the people taking part and to the society, sub-culture or group to which they belong.

Basic parameters – spirit and truth

It is clear from Scripture that worship is a priority. The Bible contains countless examples of worship by the people of God. It even contains a comprehensive hymn book in the Psalms which itself makes it clear that worship is the first calling of all creation (Psalm 150). Jesus made it clear that for him also, worship was a priority.

When talking to the woman at the well of Sychar, Jesus made it clear that God the Father was seeking worshippers who would worship in *spirit* and in *truth*:

> Yet a time is coming and has now come, when the true worshippers will worship the Father in spirit and truth, for they are the kind of worshippers the Father seeks. God is spirit and his worshippers must worship in spirit and truth (John 4:23–24).

For the Father to seek worshippers must mean that worship is one of his priorities. If it is a priority for him it must be a priority for us. In fact I would go so far as to say that worship is our first calling and our final destination. Heaven is our destination, and heaven is a place of worship. The book of Revelation reveals that worship is the primary activity of those who live in heaven. As we make worship the first concern of our lives we join all heaven in recognising God's sovereignty and lordship over all things.

Jesus said to the woman at the well that the Father is seeking a particular kind of worshipper: those who worship in spirit and in truth.

Truth in worship is maintained by establishing the primary elements of Christian worship revealed in Scripture and that have been basic to the church's worship throughout history and across the world. This is our first parameter for worship.

'Spirit' in worship is ensured by people giving themselves wholeheartedly to God, thereby expressing their wholehearted love for him. Therefore our second parameter of worship is that our worship should be accessible to those who are worshipping.

Jesus may have been referring to the Holy Spirit when he made mention of 'spirit and truth', but even if he was, he seems to have been talking about something else as well – spirit with a small 's', the human spirit. Many commentators think that he did not have the Holy Spirit in mind at all. He was referring to the worship of our spirit – our essential nature touching and being touched by God as we abandon ourselves and become vulnerable enough to worship from the very depth of our being. People being free to express themselves to God in worship allows for a vast variety. Perhaps the differences in style which are seen in every congregation everywhere in the world are something to do with people attempting to worship in spirit as well as truth.

'Truth' expresses the first of our parameters.

'Spirit' expresses the second parameter.

All Saints has gone the route of establishing an identifiable 'youth' congregation so that we can fully apply these two key principles into the life of the wider church on Brixton Hill. This may not be the best route for you. What seems to be clear, however, is that these principles need to be applied in some way.

If there is a youth group within the existing church structures, worship should still form an integral part of the meetings. Unless the priority of worship is taught from the outset by it being a vital part of the programme, the young people involved will grow up with the idea that worship is an option, and their experience of God will be cut short.

In any style or form of Christian youth work where young people are gathered together on the basis of a common faith in Jesus, worship should take place. This may seem over strong but I am certain that it is true. For me to say anything less would be a compromise on my part.

Youth worship

For congregations in Brixton, music plays an important part in worship. The music heard on the street is a closer representation of where people are and a more useful vehicle for praise and thanksgiving than the worship normally heard in church.

Even where familiar choruses and songs are sung they are re-arranged so that both musicians and congregation are able to enter in wholeheartedly.

Music that finds its roots in Africa, the Caribbean and the Black American experience are the styles most commonly used. At times this had led to new songs, known only to the congregation, being written. They may never be transferable to another context, but nevertheless accurately express the life of this particular congregation. These home-grown songs often more accurately express the life of God among us than 'imported' songs, and also reflect our faith in him.

One such song is, 'Lord bring your people home', set to an 'African' rhythm and a tune that would be at home among the singing bands of the South African townships:

Lord bring your people home,
Lord bring your people home.
Lord come and build your throne,
Lord bring your people home.

Make the desert blossom,
Make the desert green.
Rivers in the Wilderness,
Fill this land with streams.

Make a highway for us,
Open up the gates.
Level out the valleys,
Crooked paths make straight.

Turn the tears to laughter,
Sadness into joy,
Mourning into dancing,
Weak and strong employ.

Lord bring your people home,
Lord bring your people home.
Lord come and build your throne,
Lord bring your people home.

Fun in worship

'Non religious' elements are built into the worship so that it is fun and stays in touch with reality. The time of worship may include group discussions, games, videos or whatever seems appropriate to convey the particular theme for that week. These elements are not only non religious, but have an ordinariness about them which makes the worship more accessible and includes rather than excludes those who are present. Many of the games used in our school roadshows are also used in worship. We have found them particularly helpful in illustrating talks.

Making worship like this not only benefits the Christians. Worship in itself, if made accessible enough, can be a major evangelistic tool. It is when worship is an 'in house', abstract experience, only understood by Christians, that it distances those who are as yet are unfamiliar with God or worship.

Participation

The congregation are themselves encouraged to participate in the planning, preparation and leading of the worship at every level. Often a group of young people will take time during the week to work out what the worship will include and what theme will be the focus. Being able to have worship which really is their own expression of love to God means they are then able to take the risk and 'pay the price' of worshipping with other members of the church at other times.

There is a common worship time in which members from every congregation are involved. This United Service currently takes place on a Thursday evening and also involves and includes the leaders and members of other local Christian churches.

Establishing worship as a priority means that the first and most important dimension of Christian life is established within the life of individuals and the church. Worship is a priority at a congregation level, at a small group level, at an individual level and at a whole church, 'celebration' level.

From our experience at All Saints, having a time of worship specifically geared to young people seems to be an important factor in effective Christian youth work.

Fellowship and pastoral care

We have had a number of different experiences of trying to set up an adequate support structure for the young people we reach. It is one thing to find sheep, it is another to get them in a fold and start feeding them. Finding, folding and feeding need to be part of the same process so that we are able to flow naturally from one to another. The only successful method we have discovered is based on small groups. These in turn need to be a part of a larger group, which we call a congregation.

The most obvious time when the congregation is in focus is on a Sunday afternoon during the corporate worship time. The time when the small group is most clearly focussed is during the week as a number of small groups meet in people's homes. (For a more detailed explanation of small groups and congregation, see 'Pastoral Bases on Brixton Hill' in the book, *Planting New Churches*, ed Bob Hopkins, Eagle.)

Three dimensions
Our Sunday evening meetings have a primary focus on the upward dimension of worship, but even though this is the case, the 'inward' and 'outward' dimension of fellowship and service are still expressed, so that the time is fully rounded and earthed. In the same way, the small groups which are primarily focussed on fellowship need the other two dimensions to really live. Time and again our experience has been that even when an activity is focussed primarily on a single dimension, be it worship, fellowship or outreach, the activity needs to include the other two to really work.

Fig 7.1

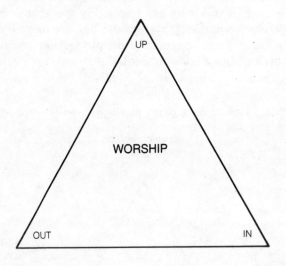

PRAISE AND THANKSGIVING

(expressed most often in music and song)

WORSHIP

UP

OUT   IN

GOING OUT

(going into the world
strengthened and
equipped for service)

SHARING

(Church sharing together
in Holy Communion giving,
prayer and bearing one
another's burdens)

Small groups – pastoral bases

Each small group should include worship, fellowship and out-reach. These three dimensions, when working together in balance, support the overall aim of fellowship, helping to give it a fuller definition in the lives of the individuals present, and keeping the group open to the possibilities of challenge and change.

Notice that in the weekly pattern (Fig 7.2 on page 120) there is provision for all the three dimensions to operate on a small and large scale. The group members get to focus on one specific dimension each time they meet, but in each activity there is the opportunity for all three dimensions to be expressed.

It is by the very fact that the fellowship group is three dimensional that fellowship and support grow. Groups which are structured in this way are less likely to become inward looking, exclusive and self interested. They are more likely to discover that a basic kingdom principle is that we receive through giving (Luke 6:38, Acts 20:35).

Fig 7.2

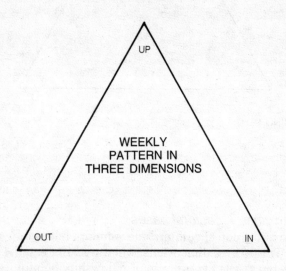

SUNDAY SERVICE

(focus on worship and word)

UP

WEEKLY
PATTERN IN
THREE DIMENSIONS

OUT

IN

A-TEAMS & WITNESS
AND SERVICE TO OTHERS

(focus on action and
application of the word)

PASTORAL BASE/
SMALL GROUP

(focus on fellowship
and understanding
the word

Individual young people can more easily be equipped to live the life of a disciple of Jesus if they are part of a small group. Group leaders are able more easily to monitor, support and encourage those going through difficulties. Also, the group itself it able to be a feeding, healing and growing environment as each member gives to the others.

Why we followed this route

I can remember the evening I walked into a youth workers' kitchen to make a cup of tea, and happened to come in on a small group of young people who had recently become Christians, meeting for fellowship around the kitchen table. Whilst making my cup of tea I was able to be a fly on the wall. As I listened in, it became clear that the young people were trying to set up a group for themselves to which only Christians were invited.

On the surface this seemed OK, except that what seemed to be coming over was that now they were Christians they had to distance themselves from their non Christian friends. In fact they seemed to be saying that this was the only way that they would grow as Christians. Initially I found myself agreeing with them as I silently made my cup of tea and went away. A few weeks later when I had had time to think, to meet the leaders and to talk to the group, it became clear that what was being proposed would end up as a rather inward looking 'youth fellowship'. All of the group had decided to leave their A-Teams so that they could concentrate on their 'Christian group' and learn how to follow Jesus. But as I pointed out, following Jesus meant more than learning a whole lot of new information with a group of likeminded people. Eventually we all agreed to jettison the idea of a 'youth fellowship' for something better that God would show us.

This incident served to show me that the tendency towards 'religion' and isolation from the world is an incredibly pervasive and powerful force. These young people had hardly become Christians before they started out in a direction that would

inevitably cut them off from their opportunities to reach out
to their contemporaries. They knew little about the need for
worship and so would have tried to develop the group simply
on the basis of fellowship – and fellowship devoid of the
upward and outward dimensions.

Small groups and congregations

To me, establishing a three dimensional life at the congre-
gational and small group level is a vital battle. As we have
taken on this commitment, the work among young people has
grown until we have now been able to plant a congregation
within the larger church of All Saints which is geared specifically to reaching and teaching them.

In the early stages of the All Saints youth project we
developed small groups like all other small groups in All
Saints, except that these were geared specifically to young
people. They were seen on equal terms with all the other
church housegroups. The groups were encouraged to be three
dimensional and a number of them grew and divided to spawn
new groups. The new congregation was planted by bringing
together two or three small groups to form a Sunday congregation. It was all a bit hit and miss, but after nearly two years
there were two evening congregations, one at 4.30 and one at
7.00, focussed on two somewhat different groups of young
people. Broadly they reach different age groups, the earlier
one reaching the eleven to seventeen age group and the later,
young adults between the ages of eighteen and thirty.

Reflecting on the whole process, I now think that although
the outcome was a good one, difficulties in defining a clear
strategy created problems. From this experience I would suggest a pattern for birthing a congregation. (See Fig 7.3 on page
123.)

This pattern is, of course, only one alternative among many.
However, the process in which a small group is part of a
congregation and the congregation is part of a larger whole
are important elements which are not merely optional.

Fig 7.3   Birthing a Congregation

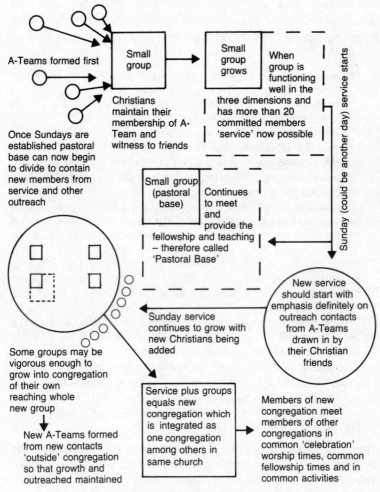

A-Teams formed first

Small group

Christians maintain their membership of A-Team and witness to friends

Small group grows

When group is functioning well in the three dimensions and has more than 20 committed members 'service' now possible

Sunday (could be another day) service starts

Once Sundays are established pastoral base can now begin to divide to contain new members from service and other outreach

Small group (pastoral base)

Continues to meet and provide the fellowship and teaching – therefore called 'Pastoral Base'

New service should start with emphasis definitely on outreach contacts from A-Teams drawn in by their Christian friends

Sunday service continues to grow with new Christians being added

Some groups may be vigorous enough to grow into congregation of their own reaching whole new group

New A-Teams formed from new contacts 'outside' congregation so that growth and outreached maintained

Service plus groups equals new congregation which is integrated as one congregation among others in same church

Members of new congregation meet members of other congregations in common 'celebration' worship times, common fellowship times and in common activities

Notice that the small group, or pastoral base, is 'outside' the new service at first, providing a 'base' for activity. Later the pastoral base divides to provide the 'infrastructure' of a new congregation. The small group begins as an exoskeleton – an outer shell – and finishes (having divided into a number of small groups) as an endoskeleton – the internal structure of the congregation

Communication

In this section we will briefly look at how to prepare talks that are really effective in getting the message of the gospel across to young people. The following story first came out in 'Street-level', All Saints' church magazine:

> My name is David Hudson, I am sixteen years old and live just a few yards from the Church, in Lyham Road.
>
> I became a Christian about three years ago so did all my friends but now all those friends have left.
>
> Before I became a Christian I used to sit around a lot. I never knew a lot of people. Martin Lee who used to work at the church invited me to join an A-Team which he ran with Bill Brannan. I became a Christian through that. I started to go to church but then dropped off.
>
> For about a year and a half after that I didn't go to church but used to hang around outside. But when it was snowing last winter and it was too cold to stay outside I went in. I saw 'enough' people throwing balls around during the service. It was supposed to be a 'Star Wars' game run by Tim Phenna. He then talked about God using the game to explain some things. That's how I started following God again. The youth services are 'safe'!
>
> Being a Christian has made an impact on my life. I have made lots of friends. I don't know how, but praying to God really helps and makes me feel better, especially when I have a problem. Mum still has to tell me to do the washing up though. I know I should help out more at home. I guess I'm just lazy.
>
> I've been asked by my mates about whether I'm a Christian or not, I've even been 'cussed' by some of them! But I'm not afraid of telling them that I am.

David is a great example of someone who has been impacted by God as he got drawn into something that he found accessible. First there was an A-Team where he made an initial response through the relationship he had with the youth workers. There was of course continuing contact with the youth team all the time he wanted to keep his distance. Then there was the service which had such an immediate effect on him and which God used to bring him close to him again.

When planning to communicate, either to a large or small group, three things need to be borne in mind. First, what do you want to say – what is the content of your message? Second, how do you want people to respond? Third, what do you need to communicate to ensure that the response is longlasting and integrated into the lifestyle of those who listen? Presented as three points for preparation they are:

1. Content
2. Response
3. Equipping

Content

Having decided the content of the message the next thing I do is to decide the best way to communicate it. I try to visualise the message in a series of pictures. The pictures can then become visual aids as I enlist the help of someone in drawing them up or using some other medium of communication, depending on what is appropriate or available.

If the message has more than one point, then each point can be prepared in this way. Even when I am not using visual aids I find this is still the best method of preparation as it provides original, graphic, verbal illustrations.

Response

When defining the response that seems to fit the message I usually go through the same process as for the content. I try to picture the response called for so that I am able to draw on my own experience of this type of response in my own life.

Of course, prayer is vital at every stage of the preparation process, but is particularly useful as we ask God to define the response. Only God really knows the response that is appropriate to his word. He is able to show us the ways in which we have responded to his word in the past and the ways we need to respond now. Often a response is called for in us who speak before any response can be expected or called for in those we speak with. Our own experience of how we have responded can be the best means of illustrating what we need to say.

Equipping

Having defined the response and decided how to communicate and illustrate it, we need to know how to end. The best way to end is to give the hearers opportunity to respond there and then and to offer a means by which they can take the message away and apply to their lives. I usually try to give one, perhaps two, practical 'things to do' (more than two often leads to confusion) and a method of working them out.

One particularly helpful approach has been to divide the group into small groups to talk through and pray for one another as they determine to put into practice what they have heard. This requires a degree of openness that may be intimidating at first. However, if the speaker has been open about his own difficulties and can use humour and sensitivity to encourage and draw others out, this method can work very well.

This method of preparation can be used for communication in any context, covering any subject. Often I have divided the message up in to 'bite sized pieces' and scattered them throughout the service, roadshow or whatever. At other times I have kept it all together and delivered the message as a single whole. Sometimes the whole frame work is a story from the Bible (a very useful approach). At other times it is a theme drawn from Scripture or everyday life. Some times brevity is important (as with an abstract theme like forgiveness); at other times time is not an issue (like when telling an interesting or funny story).

Whatever the style, length or context of the communication, this particular approach of content, response and equipping goals has always proved helpful.

In the last chapter we looked at the three dimensions of the Christian life and how they affect our youth work. I hope that this chapter has shown how the three dimensions can effect everything we do. Everything from setting up a worship service to preparing a sermon can be affected if we allow it!

Fig 7.4   How to run a small group programme

	What to remember	Notes	Timing
Welcome	Includes making new people feel comfortable and welcome		8.00
	Drinks and refreshments served		
Worship	Ask someone, probably a musician, to lead praise and singing		8.30
Prayer & sharing	Listening to God. Sharing what you think he is saying. Leaders 'weigh' word against Scripture		
Teaching/ Input	Content: What is the message? Response: What should people do? Equipping: How are you going to help them make the response – simple steps?		20–30 mins
Prayer	Pray together about what God has said		9.30
Healing	Ask God to break into people's lives in power of the kingdom		
Commission	What does God want us to do before next week?		
Informal fellowship	Drinks and food		10.00+

Leader 2			

Action extra ――――――――――――――――――

The long silence

Below is a sketch which we have often used in services. It is based on anonymous poem, 'The Long Silence'. There are, of course, many books of sketches that can be used. Writing your own, or adapting other material is often more fun and can be better tailored to your own groups' needs and, assuming you and they will be the actors, talent!

The other reason I have included this particular sketch, is that in all the time I have used drama as an evangelistic tool, it has been by far the most effective.

Narrator: At the end of time, millions of people were stretched out on the great plain before God's presence. Most shrank back from the brilliant light that was before them, but some groups, near the front, talked heatedly, not with cringing shame, but with belligerence. How can God judge us? What does he know about suffering? A young Jewish girl ripped open her sleeve to reveal an ugly number from a Nazi concentration camp: 'We endured terror, torture, beating, death'. In another group, a negro boy lowered his collar to reveal an ugly rope burn. 'What about this? Lynched for no crime but being black. We have suffered on slave ships, been wrenched from loved ones, have toiled until only death gave release'. In a third group a young man stared with sullen eyes. On his forehead was the stamp . . . 'illegitimate'. 'To endure my stigma was beyond me. Why should I suffer? It wasn't my fault.'

Each of these groups had a complaint against God for the evil and suffering he permitted in his world. 'Oh it's all right for God, living in heaven where all is sweetness and light. There's no hunger there, no hatred, no pain, no suffering, no misery, no death. What does God know about what man has to endure here on earth? God leads a pretty sheltered life.'

And so each of the groups sent out a leader, chosen because

he or she had suffered the most. There was a Jew, a negro, an untouchable from India, a horribly deformed arthritic, an illegitimate child, victims of cancer and Hiroshima, and one from a Siberian labour camp. In the centre of the plain they consulted with one another. At last they were ready to present their case . . .

During the 'sentence' one of the group becomes a symbol of Jesus, and gradually adopts a crucifix stance in response to the sentence. None of the others notice 'Jesus' behind them. Sketch now moves to dialogue between two characters – the negro boy (N) and the Jewish girl (J).

N In order for God to qualify as our judge, he must first endure what we have been forced to endure. We have decided that he must come down to earth and live as man.

J But because he is God we have set certain limitations. He must not use his divine power to save himself.

N Let *him* be born a Jew.

J Let the legitimacy of *his* birth be in doubt so that no one knows who his real father is.

N Let him be given work so difficult, that when he tries to do it even his own family think he is insane.

J Let him try to describe what no man has ever seen, felt or experienced before.

N Let him try to describe God to man.

J Let him be betrayed by his closest friends.

N Let him be convicted on false charges, tried by a prejudiced jury and condemned by a cowardly judge.

J In the end, let him know what it's like to be totally alone, completely abandoned by every living thing.

N Let him be tortured, and *let him die.*

J And let him die in such a way that there is no doubt that he is dead.

N And let there be a whole host of witnesses to verify that it is so.

Narrator: As each leader announced his portion of the sentence, loud murmurs of approval went up from the great throng assembled. But when the last had finished pronouncing the sentence . . . [they turn and notice Jesus] there was a long silence. [They kneel.]

Leaders and teams

For youth work to be effective, a church will need to gather and train a team of youth workers. If this is not possible for one church, a group of churches should do it. Team work is vital. Occasionally individual youth workers can cope alone, but this is rarely the case. An individual may, through giftedness and charisma, draw together a group of youth people, but if they have no one to support and work alongside them, invariably the work will falter and often fail. It is so sad to see very gifted youth workers become disillusioned and even give up altogether, simply through lack of support.

Whenever Jesus gave his disciples tasks, he sent them out with co-workers. This was true of the mission of the twelve (Luke 9) and the mission of the seventy-two (Luke 10), but it was also true of far simpler and more mundane tasks. When Jesus needed a donkey to ride on or a room to meet in, he sent out more than one disciple to complete the task. It would seem that the smallest working unit in the kingdom is two.

Jesus was the team leader par excellence. He, above all others, knew how to gather, train and build a team. His objective in doing this was to get them ready to take on his mission and his ministry to the world.

What follows is a method of team building which I have used for a number of years with many different teams. The principles are drawn from my understanding of Jesus as a team leader. These principles can be used in a number of different ways, for instance in the training of individual leaders (see my book, *Growing the Smaller Church*, CPAS Marshall Pickering (1992), but here they will be applied almost exclusively to the gathering, training and building of a team of youth workers.

Vision

A team is a group of people working together with a common vision. In calling people to join a team we must be absolutely clear about two things. The first is the general vision that we have for the work of the team. The second is what the particular individuals we are calling could do to help fulfil that vision.

Jesus' preaching of the kingdom can be summarised in the statement, 'The time has come, the kingdom of God is near, repent and believe the good news' (Mark 1:15). This was the vision that motivated him and the one which he called others to share in. But he also had a particular task in mind for his team members. For Peter and Andrew, this was, 'Come follow me and I will make you fishers of men' (Mark 1:17). The fishermen were able to respond and immediately follow Jesus because he gave them a vision and a way that they could fit into it.

When contemplating starting a youth team it is important the task always follows the vision. In this way our work will always be *led* by God and not *driven* by desire. Knowing what to do is important but knowing where you are going is even more important. Jesus first gave the vision and then defined the task.

Vision and leadership

When defining a vision, leadership is essential; when forming any team, leadership is vital. To form a team around a vision means we must begin with finding a leader with a vision.

In most situations this will mean that the church leadership, or joint church leadership, finds one person who may, or may not be a full time worker, and delegates the task of team leadership. If the task of team leadership is delegated to one person, the church leaders need first to be clear about their vision and then be prepared to say what they expect. Task follows vision.

Having heard the general vision, the prospective team leader needs to take the vision to God in prayer to ask him to make the vision personal and real to them. The potential team leader will need to return to the church leaders with any new ideas or insight to help clarify the vision still further. It is important that there is an agreement on the overall vision at this stage. Everyone needs to be pulling in the same direction. Care and time taken at this stage will be of enormous benefit later. If problems occur, everyone can return to the shared vision of a starting point in solving the problems and planning for the future.

Problems arise when church leaders set a youth worker to work only to find that what is being done does not fulfil their expectations or express their vision. Problems like this can so easily be avoided if care is taken at the outset.

For a vision to be clear it needs to contain a number of things. There will need to be an understanding of a basic need which God is highlighting and an urgency to see God meet it. For instance, young people with nothing to do falling prey to vandalism, crime and drugs would be a specific need.

There will also need to be an expression of urgency and an expectation that God will meet these needs. God breaking in, rescuing, redeeming and rebuilding lives would be God meeting the need and providing a solution.

The vision will usually include a basic strategy. For instance, young people brought into an experience of God's transforming power through relationships of commitment and trust, is a basic strategy.

As well as this, the vision may have special characteristics that make it real for a particular group of people in a particular place at a particular time. For instance, a number of youth projects were established in the Brixton area soon after and in response to the riots of April 1981.

Once the vision is sufficiently clear it can be communicated to other people, and the church leaders can release the youth team leader to gather a team.

Defining a vision and settling who the leader is means that a plan can be made. Although planning is a corporate activity which should eventually be shared across the whole team, in the early stages of a team's life much of the plan will need to be worked on by church leaders and the team leader.

Team building: Stage I – Getting going
The key at this stage is to find people who share the vision, not just people who are good or experienced youth workers. If someone joins the team who does not share the vision, problems will inevitably surface; this is true even if they are the best youth worker you can find.

Often, fulfilling a vision will require learning new methods – new way of doing things – and sometimes people 'with experience' are the most resistant to these new ways. No doubt there were many excellent teachers and communicators among the scribes and pharisees in Jesus' day, but their experience prevented them from becoming effective disciples. They were old wineskins that could not contain the new wine (Mark 2:22). This does not always have to be the case; some experienced youth workers will share your vision and will be humble enough to learn new methods. Whatever the case, it is vital to gather a team around a vision rather than anything else.

The team leader
In the early stages of a team's life it will be important to establish who the leader is and how the leadership operates. Leaders need to be followers first, servants second and leaders last if they are to model a biblical pattern of leadership. But following the Lord and his direction and being the servant of others does not mean that a leader can duck the responsibility to direct and guide others. Directive leadership is not particularly liked in some circles, but is absolutely essential in the early stages of a team's life. Clear vision and a clear lead need to be maintained.

If the team leader is a humble person who submits to the authority of the church leaders and is accountable for what they say and do, they will inspire confidence in others. Others will be prepared to follow a leader like this.

Tasks given

Gathering a team around a clear vision means that individual tasks can be given out. It is probably good that everyone gets to do a bit of everything. Even if the specification of each team member's role is clear, everyone should still have time to be exposed to all the work. This is a stretching experience for everyone and gives the opportunity to reveal unknown strengths and weaknesses. In time roles will no doubt become more defined, but this should not happen too quickly.

Team disciplines

As well as individual tasks given to the different members of the team, specific team disciplines need to be built into the programme at this stage. These include:

(a) Learning to keep a work diary. Keeping appointments may not come naturally to some people; being on time can also be a problem. Keeping some sort of appointment diary can help with both.

(b) Learning to review work. At times we have used report sheets which can be filled out after each A-Team session. These can be particularly helpful in improving awareness and basic relationship skills. They can contain the following type of checklist:

A-Team prayer and review sheet

A-Team name:
Date of activity:
Attendance:
Activity planned on the programme:
Activity done (if different from above):
Matters arising from last week:
Specific objective for activity this week:

Group dynamics

Did the group work well together?
Were they happy and confident?

Are there any individuals needing special attention?
How well did you relate to the group?
Was your style of leadership appropriate?
Were you sensitive to needs in the group?

Encouragements and problems

	Encouraging things	Particular problems
Leader 1		
Leader 2		

Specific objects for next week:

Ideas for future action
Group:
Individuals:

REMEMBER: Use 'Specific Objectives' for prayer throughout the week. These sheets should be returned to the team leader. Be sure to talk through any worries or concerns with your team leader.

At a time of worship, prayer, Bible study and fellowship is essential if the team is to maintain its focus and to stay open to God and his direction. By establishing the priority of worship within the team, the team will be able to live out a three dimensional life. The upward is expressed in worship and prayer, the inward dimension in fellowship and teamwork, and the outward dimension in the tasks that the team takes on (see chapter six). The team should meet at least once a week. Where possible, particularly if teams have full or part timers who work together on a daily basis, some form of daily discipline of corporate prayer is invaluable. These disciplines provide the backbone and stability for a team's life. When problems or difficulties arise, disciplines such as these help you through.

Summary

The team will be enthusiastic, but inexperienced, highly confident, but low in competence. The leader needs to provide clear direction through a clearly communicated vision. He also needs to be directive in assigning tasks and pointing the way to getting the work done. This may be an unfamiliar, even unpopular style of leadership in some circles. Even the term 'classical leadership' used to describe this style make it seem a little out of date. However, this style is essential in the first stages of the team's life.

Fig 8.1

STAGE IV	STAGE III

STAGE I
 	
TEAM: HIGH ENTHUSIASM
         LOW EXPERIENCE
         HIGH CONFIDENCE
         LOW COMPETENCE
 	
LEADER: HIGH ON DIRECTION
         LOW ON CONSENSUS
         HIGH ON EXAMPLE
         LOW ON EXPLANATION
 	
Jesus: Mark 1:15–18
Basic leadership style: directive/classical
	STAGE II

Team building: Stage II – Growing up

The second stage of team building is important because it is often the make or break stage. The team has begun to do the work, and individuals have been given particular tasks. The enthusiasm and commitment of the team will usually not be matched by their competence to do the work. How many times have youth workers new to the work rushed in where angels fear to tread!

I can remember, as a fresh faced youth worker just out of college, giving my first 'Christian talk' to a group of East End kids on the Hackney Marshes. Even though the subject was quite a serious one, most of the group were laughing hysterically by the time I was half way through. I tried to ignore this obvious distraction when it was just one or two giggling and nudging each other, but finally, when even the ones who wanted to concentrate were laughing, in desperation I stopped and I asked one of them what they were all laughing at. He dried his eyes and controlled himself just enough to tell me that in the local lingo, some of the words that I had used were highly sexually explicit! The initial shock that a Christian youth worker would use such words gave way to the hilarity as I used them again and again. When I had recovered from the embarrassment, and had a good laugh myself, I asked one or two of them to teach me the 'local' language and tell me whenever I slipped up again. I was an enthusiastic communicator, but not very competent one!

Team leader as coach

To develop another person's skills as a youth worker does not mean that you have to be a highly competent youth worker yourself. It simply means that you have an ability to 'coach' other people. At times I have been only half a step ahead of new youth workers as I have trained them. The talents of some have been such that today many are much better youth workers than I am. A coach usually knows how to recognise unhelpful, unproductive behaviour, and knows what needs to be done to rectify this behaviour and how to begin to develop better behaviour. For instance, a football coach will see a footballer kicking the ball with the end of his toe. He will take the player aside and point out that kicking the ball in this way means the player will have little control over the ball. He will then show the player how to push the ball with the inside of the foot for accurate passing and kick the ball with the upper part of the foot for accurate shooting.

In youth work the problem may be how the youth worker communicates with the young people, how they maintain discipline, or how they solve problems that the young people present. Whatever the problem, the team leader will need to coach the workers through the problems that a lack of experience and competence create. To be a coach means working on a day to day basis alongside those you lead, in an informal way. But it may also require some formal pattern of monitoring and assessment.

Monitoring and assessment

Half an hour set aside each week with each individual to talk through problems and help with new ideas has proved invaluable for me in the past. Teams I have led have called this the weekly 'on-line' session. If a weekly meeting is impossible, then at least one hour a month should be given to each team member. Skills training needs to be continuous, taken at a steady pace with lots of time given to the process.

Having these regular reviews fulfils one of the key objectives of this stage, which is for the youth workers to learn how to monitor themselves. Making the 'learning loop' part of their everyday lives is important at this stage (see chapter four). Once a year an 'MOT' is usually needed. This is a time when a worker can assess their own development and growth, and make plans for the coming year. The yearly review sheet is included in the practical section at the end of the chapter.

I have used a simple self assessment 'score sheet' which, as long as it is used in a light hearted way, can be a useful means of helping team members keep a focus on developing as a youth worker and growing as a person. It is best used as a regular review tool. (See Fig 8.5 on page 151.)

Job description

Working with team members on their personal job description at this stage can be enormously beneficial. Of course it will need fairly constant review but this is often the time when it can have the greatest effect. Writing the description earlier is unnecessary – it doesn't tend to mean much to someone new to the work. It can also be unwise – it is probably better to let the work define itself and let the team members discover what the work *means* before we tie down what they *do*.

A-Team leader's job description

Our overall aim is to see young people in the community become Christian disciples in every area of their lives and integrated into All Saints Church.

We aim to help young people take responsibility for their own lives.

We aim to do this by building good quality friendships and not by 'providing' a service for 'clients'.

Therefore an 'A-Team' worker needs to:

1. Make friends with the young people in your group.

2. Pray for your A-Team regularly, both personally, with your co-leader and with your house group.

3. Help the young people to take responsibility for their own lives, assisting in their growth to maturity.

4. Demonstrate the kingdom of God through loving action, and when appropriate, explain the good news of the kingdom of God.

5. Help the young people to be integrated into All Saints Church either through a house group or by coming to a Sunday service.

6. Meet in your home or theirs outside group time.

7. Keep an awareness of the group's dynamics.
8. Learn to apply appropriate leadership skills.
9. Work closely with other group leaders.
10. Fill in a weekly review sheet.
11. Attend organised training events.
12. Become a member of a housegroup.
13. Regularly attend church services.
14. Work under the oversight of your team leader/s and the church leadership.

Dealing with discouragement as a coach

Realising there is so much to learn can often lead to discouragement, and a continual awareness of incompetence tends to dishearten.

The crucial role of the leader is to continue to envision, by reminding the team of the vision that first drew them together and by praising them and encouraging them for every sign of growth or improvement. A good leader and coach seeks to build up the team, recognising that a discouraged team is often an ineffective one. The outstanding little book, *The One Minute Manager*, suggests that leaders should spend a good part of their time trying to catch their team doing well and praising them publicly for it. Although sometimes correction will be needed, this should be private; praise, as far as possible, should be public.

If correction is needed, the team leader needs to make it clear that he still approves of the team member and that the basis of their relationship is not how well they perform, but that they both belong to Jesus Christ. Leaders needs to be bold and courageous and correct their team when necessary. This should be as an expression of their love, not an expression of their frustration. It is important to develop an approach towards correction that strengthens relationships rather than weakens them.

Jesus was a coach to his team. He could often be seen correcting, praising, encouraging the disciples along the way. As they went from the extremes of success to failure, Jesus continued to present the vision of the kingdom. Most of his ministry was spent working alongside the disciples, showing them how to live like him and preparing them for the time when he would delegate to them the responsibilities of his mission and ministry.

Failure can often reveal problems in our self image. If we have learned, through an experience of receiving *conditional* love, that the approval of others and our value is based on how well we do, failure will be a big problem. Team leaders will need to constantly remind their team of the gospel of grace. God's love is always *unconditional*. He loved us even when we were still sinners and still does. As his children we can be sure that God continues to love us just as much as he ever did. He is our Father and he approves of and highly values his children, not because of what they do, but because they are his.

Christians sometimes forget the grace that saved them and sustains them. The 'works' that could not gain God's approval before we became Christians still do not convince him to approve of us. He already approves of us; he hates our sin but loves us completely and unconditionally always. As we focus on developing a person's skills and abilities as a youth worker, we need to guard against the idea, so prevalent in some strands of Christianity, that doing well leads to approval. Our love and approval should be like God's – unconditional. This does not mean that correction and praise are not appropriate. Simply that whatever we have to say to our teams they should not destroy, rather build up.

Summary
At stage two of the training process, the team may begin to run into the sand! Problems, which lack of competence and experience create, cause difficulties. A drop in confidence and enthusiasm is a natural result.

The leader needs to coach the team through the problems,

concentrating his effort on spending time with the team members. He will need to remind the team of the initial vision, and through simple steps lead people out of failure into a growing competence and increased confidence in themselves, and more particularly, in the God who has called them. He needs to continue to be clear and directive, but plenty of discussion should be encouraged and everyone should know that he is available to spend time talking through their problems.

Fig 8.2

STAGE IV	STAGE III
STAGE I	**STAGE II**
TEAM: HIGH ENTHUSIASM LOW EXPERIENCE HIGH CONFIDENCE LOW COMPETENCE	**TEAM:** LOW ENTHUSIASM LOW EXPERIENCE LOW CONFIDENCE LOW COMPETENCE
LEADER: HIGH ON DIRECTION LOW ON CONSENSUS HIGH ON EXAMPLE LOW ON EXPLANATION	**LEADER:** HIGH ON DIRECTION HIGH ON DISCUSSION HIGH ON EXAMPLE HIGH ON ACCESSIBILITY
Jesus: Mark 1:15–18 Basic leadership style: directive/classical	Jesus: Luke 12:31–32 Basic leadership style: coach/charismatic

Team building: Stage III – Growing together

If stage one can be described as 'getting going', stage two as 'growing up', then stage three is about 'growing together'. At this stage the team becomes the primary focus. *Reporting* on how we were doing becomes *supporting* one another in what we are doing. Time spent together is at a premium. Days away, weekend retreats, even team holidays all help to underline the focus of growing together.

Specific team building events like shared meals on a regular basis are valuable at this stage. Learning from one another's skills and experience by sharing in one another's work is also helpful. As the team grows in confidence and the relationships become more mutually supportive, the team becomes a good place to explore and understand more about our weaknesses and strengths. A good team leader will be wanting to identify those who at this stage can be groomed to lead their own teams, and others who can be encouraged towards taking more responsibility in particular areas of work. Corporate worship, prayer and teaching are important at every stage, but at this stage they take on a life of their own. Greater portions of time can be given to these things as the team learns to relax in the company of one another and in the presence of God.

Towards the end of his ministry, Jesus gives us an excellent example of a stage three leader. His teaching at the last supper, emphasising unity, equality and the maintenance of relationships through service and sacrificial love, are key elements in his teaching.

Failures in Stage III

Broken or strained relationships can be concentrated on during this phase of a team's life. Time should be given to allow the hurts to heal and the relationships to be restored as the disciplines of forgiveness and accountability are to be applied.

Occasionally a major failure or personal disaster in the life of a team member can lead to that person crashing back down to stage two. The team leader needs to learn how to respond to this. In doing this I have taken my inspiration from the model of restoration found when Jesus restored Peter (John 21).

Peter, having denied Christ three times is now in the pit of depression, even though Jesus has been raised from the dead. To restore him Jesus takes him back to his first experience of discipleship – the miraculous haul of fishes (John 21:1–6). He confronts him with reality, using a charcoal fire like the one that Peter stood warming himself around as he denied him (John 18:25). He calls him to recognise the primary place of their relationship by asking, 'Do you love me' (John 21:17). He illuminates the task of leadership – 'Feed my sheep' – and calls him back into discipleship and as a member of the team when he says, 'Come follow me' (John 21:19).

Failures and disasters in our work can come in large or small packages. Once one of the female workers on our youth team turned up at a church leaders' meeting in a distraught state. At first we couldn't work out what had happened because she was almost completely incoherent as she tried to talk between the sobs. Eventually we got the story.

She had been having a Bible study with a group of girls in the church building and had made the mistake of leaving the door unlocked. A group of older teenage boys that we had had some contact with came in, probably looking for something to do. When she asked them to leave, explaining that she was having a Bible study, they said no, and said they would stay and listen. Not wishing to deal with a possible confrontation she let them stay and they were completely disruptive. Rather too late in the day she decided to stand her ground and tell them to go. They stood their ground too. They left only after threatening her and telling her they would be waiting for her on the way home. Knowing the boys were fully capable of fulfilling their threats she got scared, prayed with her group, walked them home and then ran as fast as she could, thinking she was being followed, to the leaders' meeting.

When she reached the leaders' meeting she was ready to give up her job, move house, leave the area, the whole lot! Not much of the business that was planned for the leaders' meeting got done that night. Instead I, and a couple of others, spent our time listening to the story and helping her re-focus on why she was a youth worker and a member of the team. We helped to recall how she knew God had called her and what she was going to do to sort out this problem.

Later in the week when she and I went with her to see the boys, amazingly they apologised. They were surprised that anybody followed through, and wanted to resolve the situation. This was something they had not experienced before. The whole experience, though fairly minor by comparison with others we have seen, was one in which God was able to break in to restore and rebuild.

Jesus the flexible leader

As you can see from the material in this chapter, leadership is a complex business. Jesus was a flexible leader able to respond to people at different stages of their development. His initial style was highly directive, then he was a coach holding the vision of the kingdom before his struggling disciples. Next he was a counsellor focussing all his attention on relationships as the basis for future delegation. Finally he was a delegating leader concentrating on his team taking on the vision themselves and understanding the plan and the method of review.

Summary

The team are now growing together and spending a lot of time with each other. The team's needs will vary greatly from day to day and so the leader will need to be fluid, responsive and relationship centred. Coaching has improved the team member's ability to work effectively and so confidence has begun to rise. The leader will need to continue to spend a lot of time with the team, coaching them through their difficulties. But now he will be giving them more opportunity to take personal responsibility for their work. Decision making will become more by consensus, with the relationship in the team taking priority over the task.

Fig 8.3

STAGE IV	STAGE III
	TEAM: INCREASING ENTHUSIASM GROWING EXPERIENCE INTERMITTENT CONFIDENCE GROWING COMPETENCE **LEADER:** LOWER ON DIRECTION HIGHER ON CONSENSUS HIGH ON DISCUSSION HIGH ON ASSESSIBILITY Jesus: John 15:1–8 Basic leadership style: human relations/consensus
STAGE I	**STAGE II**
TEAM: HIGH ENTHUSIASM LOW EXPERIENCE HIGH CONFIDENCE LOW COMPETENCE **LEADER:** HIGH ON DIRECTION LOW ON CONSENSUS HIGH ON EXAMPLE LOW ON EXPLANATION Jesus: Mark 1:15–18 Basic leadership style: directive/classical	**TEAM:** LOW ENTHUSIASM LOW EXPERIENCE LOW CONFIDENCE LOW COMPETENCE **LEADER:** HIGH ON DIRECTION HIGH ON DISCUSSION HIGH ON EXAMPLE HIGH ON ACCESSIBILITY Jesus: Luke 12:31–32 Basic leadership style: coach/charismatic

Team building: Stage IV – Going out

Eventually the team will have developed to the stage where some members will now be ready to leave, sent out with the task of leading their own teams. Others will be sufficiently trained to take up more responsible positions within the team, perhaps heading up one area of the work. At this stage the team leader needs to concentrate on ensuring that each team member knows how to plan and review and is able to spend longer periods of time working without direct oversight. The leader will need to ensure that each team member is able to maintain the original vision, the principles of team work, and now they are more competent, continue to maintain supportive relationships with other members of the team.

Team members will now be competent youth workers and confident enough to work without the team leader constantly looking on. This does not mean that suddenly the team divides into a team of individuals. Less time is needed to maintain relationships because they have grown to a measure of maturity through the previous three stages. The team is now built around relationships that should last a lifetime, strong enough to endure this new phase when team members will tend to spend less time together.

As some leave to answer the call of God to do new things in new locations the team will experience a loss. But it need not disrupt the team completely. New members can be brought in and the team can begin the process of development that leads to confident and competent youth workers. This time around more people know what they are doing, and so when team members work in pairs perhaps one of the experienced workers can take on another less experienced person. The 'old hand' works alongside the new team member, taking them through the four stages themselves. This ensures that two things are achieved: first the new person is trained, and second the older team member reviews what they have learned.

Team leaders can get discouraged at this stage, seeing their team members leave for new locations and a whole new team needing just as much input coming together. But this is part and parcel of team leadership and needs to be recognised by the team leader at the outset. The sense of bereavement experienced by the team leader and older team members as others leave may be very deep and very real, but if you are ready and prepared it should not last too long.

For me one of the great challenges in leadership is that you know many of your current team will not be with you in a few years' time and that you will be back to square one (or stage one) in just a short time. But this is more than compensated for when you realise that you have the opportunity of really influencing the lives of some. A sense of privilege and gratitude grows to take the place of any sadness or loss.

Fig 8.4

STAGE IV	STAGE III
TEAM: HIGH ENTHUSIASM HIGH EXPERIENCE HIGH CONFIDENCE HIGH COMPETENCE **LEADER:** LOW ON DIRECTION HIGH ON CONSENSUS LOW ON EXAMPLE HIGH ON DELEGATION Jesus: Matthew 28:18–20 Basic leadership style: non directive/ delegating	**TEAM:** INCREASING ENTHUSIASM GROWING EXPERIENCE INTERMITTENT CONFIDENCE GROWING COMPETENCE **LEADER:** LOWER ON DIRECTION HIGHER ON CONSENSUS HIGH ON DISCUSSION HIGH ON ACCESSIBILITY Jesus: John 15:1–8 Basic leadership style: human relations/ consensus
STAGE I	STAGE II
TEAM: HIGH ENTHUSIASM LOW EXPERIENCE HIGH CONFIDENCE LOW COMPETENCE **LEADER:** HIGH ON DIRECTION LOW ON CONSENSUS HIGH ON EXAMPLE LOW ON EXPLANATION Jesus: Mark 1:15–18 Basic leadership style: directive/classical	**TEAM:** LOW ENTHUSIASM LOW EXPERIENCE LOW CONFIDENCE LOW COMPETENCE **LEADER:** HIGH ON DIRECTION HIGH ON DISCUSSION HIGH ON EXAMPLE HIGH ON ACCESSIBILITY Jesus: Luke 12:31–32 Basic leadership style: coach/charismatic

Summary
The team is now highly confident and competent, able to maintain its own momentum and enthusiasm and sufficiently experienced to begin taking on areas of delegation.

The leader needs to release authority to the team, delegating responsibility to them for their calling as youth workers.

Regular contact to plan and review is necessary, but relationships within the team should be at a stage where they can maintain themselves without much external input.

GET GOING! —————————————————————

It is clear from this chapter that a team leader needs to exercise different styles of leadership at different times. This in itself is a real challenge to those contemplating leading a team. But if we do not know where we are strong in our leadership style and where we are weak, we will find it difficult to be effective and have little idea of where to concentrate our effort in learning new things.

Star graph and personal assessment
The star graph, along with the leadership activity score sheet and the four boxes which outline various leadership styles, are tools for revealing our strengths and weaknesses as leaders. The personal assessment and review sheet which follows is intended as a yearly review tool which should first be used by a leader before others try it.

Ideally you should end up with an even circle (see example graph one). This will indicate that you are a good all round leader. What usually happens is one or two quarters show a higher score than the others (see example graph two). This highlights the particular styles of leadership where the leader is either strong or weak.

The score is less important than making a circle. The objective is to develop a balanced and rounded approach to leadership which can flexibly respond to different people at different times. Flexible leaders who can operate in different styles of leadership is what is needed to take people through to a stage where delegation can take place.

Fig 8.5

Give yourself a score out of ten for the following leadership activities:

Graph no.	Leadership activity	1 2 3 4 Current Score	5 6 7 Term's Target	8 9 10 Year's Target
11	Meeting the needs of others			
1	Decision making			
15	Delegating your work to others			
12	Enabling others to do their work			
2	Detailed planning			
3	Controlling situations/organising others			
10	Recognising needs in people & situations			
14	Development/Growth of others			
8	Making people feel good about themselves			
4	Taking initiative in 'crisis'			
6	Communicate your feelings clearly			
9	Working with others on shared project			
7	Communicate plans and ideas			
5	Taking initiative in day-to-day situation			
13	Discovering ways of making situations/people/projects work better			
16	Thinking and planning ahead 1 month ahead score . . .* 6 months ahead score . . .* 1 year ahead score . . .* 5 years ahead score . . .* *add these scores together and divide by four to find current score*			

Fig 8.6   The star graph

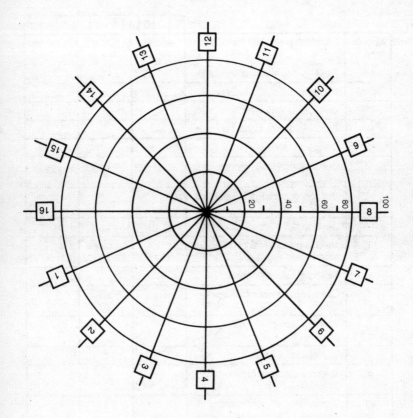

Fig 8.7   The star graph – example 1

Outside In

Fig 8.8 The star graph – example 2

If we place the boxes and star graph together, each leadership style is revealed in its place on the graph. We can see how effective we are in each area of leadership. If we are clearly down in one area it will give us something to concentrate on as we grow as youth workers and leaders.

Fig 8.9   Star graph with boxes

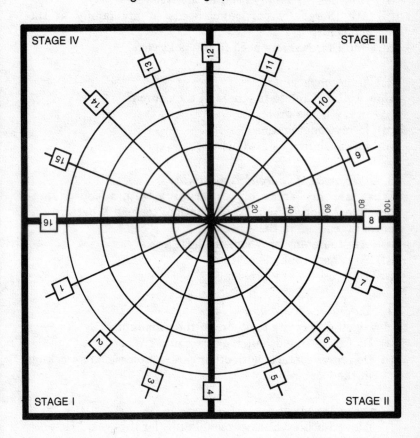

Personal assessment and review
Name:
Job title:
Job description:

1. *Family*
Family (spouse, children, parents, brothers/sisters).
(i) How has my family been in the last year?
(ii) Are there any particular needs in my family at the moment?
(iii) Can I foresee any need in the next year?

2. *Church membership*
How well do I relate to others in the church?
(i) in my house group
(ii) in my congregation
(iii) in the church as a whole

3. *Other areas of church responsibility*
What are my areas of responsbility within church programmes? (house group, congregation, teams). What are the encouragements in these areas?
(i) Are there any problems in these areas?
(ii) Are there conflicts of time?
(iii) Do I foresee any problems?

4. *You and the community*
How well do I relate to others in the community?
(i) Do I have friends outside the church? Who?
(ii) Do I have contacts with other carers/professionals working in the locality?

5. *Work assessment*
(i) Have I achieved my personal aims for this year? How?
(ii) Have I achieved the aims given me by others this year? How?

(iii) How has my work supported the overall work of the church?
(iv) Do I feel satisfied and fulfilled in my work?
(v) Do I need further training in any particular areas?
(vi) Do I feel that my work is really worthwhile? Why?

6. *Team work*
(i) How well do I relate to others on the full time team?
(ii) Are there particular people with whom I have to work harder at a better relationship? How?
(iii) How do I work alongside others in my area of work?
(iv) How do I work alongside others in their area of work?

7. *Work in the coming year*
Where do I hope to be next year with my work?
(i) Do I have a clear aim for my areas of responsibility for 1990? What?
(ii) Do I have a plan of how to achieve this aim?
(iii) Is this aim clearly communicated to others involved in that area of work?

8. *Obstacles in the coming year*
Are there obstacles that I can forsee next year?
(i) Personal relationships in team
(ii) Personal relationships in church
(iii) Personal relationships in family
(iv) Training needs

9. *Problems and needs*
Can I foresee any personal and practical needs?
(i) Housing
(ii) Money
(iii) Transport
(iv) Holidays
(v) Major life changes (marriage, death in family, etc)

10. *Any other business!*
Do I have anything to say to church leaders/pastors?

Fig 8.10

Give yourself a score out of ten for the following leadership activities:

Graph no.	Leadership activity	Current Score 1 2 3			Term's Target 4 5 6 7				Year's Target 8 9 10		
11	Meeting the needs of others										
1	Decision making										
15	Delegating your work to others										
12	Enabling others to do their work										
2	Detailed planning										
3	Controlling situations/organising others										
10	Recognising needs in people & situations										
14	Development/Growth of others										
8	Making people feel good about themselves										
4	Taking initiative in 'crisis'										
6	Communicate your feelings clearly										
9	Working with others on shared project										
7	Communicate plans and ideas										
5	Taking initiative in day-to-day situation										
13	Discovering ways of making situations/people/projects work better										
16	Thinking and planning ahead 1 month ahead score . . .* 6 months ahead score . . .* 1 year ahead score . . .* 5 years ahead score . . .* *add these scores together and divide by four to find current score*										

Epilogue

You may be wondering where to start. The answer to that is back at chapter one. Begin by trying to understand young people and the culture of which they are a part. Learn how to communicate, understand their needs, think through how to apply the gospel – good news to their bad news – and find others with a similar desire. Together ask God to bring together a team – at least two – who will hear God on how to reach out to young people and seek to bring them within the fold of the local church. Starting small is a good place to start. Allow God to show you your first 'person of peace', and your first contact peer group. Remember to fight to stay clear of 'providing' a programme and getting them 'in church', and concentrate on relationships which lead to Jesus being seen in your life. Then the kingdom which starts as a small mustard seed will begin to grow. And grow it must because God's commitment to young people is unconditional. We need only tap into his heart's desire is to show his love for them, to see kingdom growth begin. If we go and take the message and the methods of the gospel given in Scripture, the tiny seed will become a mighty tree.